A
Semantic
Web
Primer

# A
# Semantic
# Web
# Primer

Grigoris Antoniou

and

Frank van Harmelen

The MIT Press
Cambridge, Massachusetts
London, England

This book was set in 10/13 Palatino by the authors using LATEX $2_\varepsilon$.
Printed and bound in the United States of America.

Library of Congress Cataloging-in-Publication Data

Antoniou, G. (Grigoris)
        A semantic Web primer/ Grigoris Antoniou and Frank van Harmelen.
                p.    cm.–(Cooperative information systems)
        Includes bibliographical references and index.
        ISBN 0-262-01210-3 (hc.: alk. paper)
        1. Semantic Web. I. Van Harmelen, Frank. II. Title. III. Series.
TK5105.88815. A58   2004
025.04–dc22
                                                          2003065165

    10  9  8  7  6  5  4  3  2

*Dedicated to Konstantina*

G.A.

# Brief Contents

# Contents

# List of Figures

# Series Foreword

The traditional view of information systems as tailor-made, cost-intensive database applications is changing rapidly. The change is fueled partly by a maturing software industry, which is making greater use of off-the-shelf generic components and standard software solutions, and partly by the onslaught of the information revolution. In turn, this change has resulted in a new set of demands for information services that are homogeneous in their presentation and interaction patterns, open in their software architecture, and global in their scope. The demands have come mostly from application domains such as e-commerce and banking, manufacturing (including the software industry itself), training, education, and environmental management, to mention just a few.

Future information systems will have to support smooth interaction with a large variety of independent multi-vendor data sources and legacy applications, running on heterogeneous platforms and distributed information networks. Metadata will play a crucial role in describing the contents of such data sources and in facilitating their integration.

As well, a greater variety of community-oriented interaction patterns will have to be supported by next-generation information systems. Such interactions may involve navigation, querying and retrieval, and will have to be combined with personalized notification, annotation, and profiling mechanisms. Such interactions will also have to be intelligently interfaced with application software, and will need to be dynamically integrated into customized and highly connected cooperative environments. Moreover, the massive investments in information resources, by governments and businesses alike, call for specific measures that ensure security, privacy and accuracy of their contents.

All these are challenges for the next generation of information systems. We call such systems *Cooperative Information Systems*, and they are the focus of this series.

In lay terms, cooperative information systems are servicing a diverse mix of demands characterized by *content—community—commerce*. These demands are originating in current trends for off-the-shelf software solutions, such as enterprise resource planning and e-commerce systems.

A major challenge in building cooperative information systems is to develop technologies that permit continuous enhancement and evolution of current massive investments in information resources and systems. Such technologies must offer an appropriate infrastructure that supports not only development, but also evolution of software.

Early research results on cooperative information systems are becoming the core technology for community-oriented information portals or gateways. An information gateway provides a "one-stop-shopping" place for a wide range of information resources and services, thereby creating a loyal user community.

The research advances that will lead to cooperative information systems will not come from any single research area within the field of Information Technology. Database and knowledge-based systems, distributed systems, groupware, and graphical user interfaces have all matured as technologies. While further enhancements for individual technologies are desirable, the greatest leverage for technological advancement is expected to come from their evolution into a seamless technology for building and managing cooperative information systems.

The MIT Press Cooperative Information Systems series will cover this area through textbooks, and research editions intended for the researcher and the professional who wishes to remain up-to-date on current developments and future trends.

The series will include three types of books:

- Textbooks or resource books intended for upper level undergraduate or graduate level courses;

- Research monographs, which collect and summarize research results and development experiences over a number of years;

- Edited volumes, including collections of papers on a particular topic.

Data in a data source are useful because they model some part of the real world, its subject matter (or *application*, or *domain of discourse*). The problem of *data semantics* is establishing and maintaining the correspondence between a data source, hereafter a *model*, and its intended subject matter. The model may be a database storing data about employees in a company, a database schema describing parts, projects and suppliers, a Web site presenting information about a university, or a plain text file describing the battle of Waterloo. The problem has been with us since the development of the first databases. However, the problem remained under control as long as the operational environment of a database remained closed and relatively stable. In such a setting, the meaning of the data was factored out from the database proper and entrusted to the small group of regular users and application programs.

The advent of the Web has changed all that. Databases today are made available, in some form, on the Web where users, application programs, and uses are open-ended and ever changing. In such a setting, the semantics of the data has to be made available along with the data. For human users, this is done through an appropriate choice of presentation format. For application programs, however, this semantics has to be provided in a formal and machine processable form. Hence the call for the Semantic Web.[1]

Not surprisingly, this call by Tim Berners-Lee has received tremendous attention by researchers and practitioners alike. There is now an International Semantic Web Conference series,[2] a Web Semantic Journal published by Elsevier,[3] as well as industrial committees that are looking at the first generation of standards for the Semantic Web.

The current book constitutes a timely publication, given the fast-moving nature of Semantic Web concepts, technologies, and standards. The book offers a gentle introduction to Semantic Web concepts, including XML, DTDs, and XML schemas, RDF and RDFS, OWL, Logic, and Inference. Throughout, the book includes examples and applications to illustrate the use of concepts.

We are pleased to include this book on the Semantic Web in the series on Cooperative Information Systems. We hope that readers will find it interesting, insightful, and useful.

John Mylopoulos
jm@cs.toronto.edu
Dept. of Computer Science
University of Toronto
Toronto, Ontario
Canada

Michael Papazoglou
M.P.Papazoglou@kub.nl
INFOLAB
P.O. Box 90153
LE Tilburg
The Netherlands

---

1. Tim Berners-Lee and Mark Fischetti, *Weaving the Web: The Original Design and Ultimate Destiny of the World Wide Web by Its Inventor* (San Francisco: HarperCollins, 1999).
2. <http://iswc.semanticweb.org>
3. <http://www.semanticwebjournal.org>

# *Preface*

The World Wide Web (WWW) has changed the way people communicate with each other, how information is disseminated and retrieved, and how business is conducted. The term *Semantic Web* comprises techniques that promise to dramatically improve the current WWW and its use. This book is about this emerging technology.

The success of each book should be judged against the authors' aims. This is an introductory textbook about the Semantic Web. Its main use will be to serve as the basis for university courses about the Semantic Web. It can also be used for self -study by anyone who wishes to learn about Semantic Web technologies.

The question arises whether there is a need for a textbook, given that all information is available online. We think there is a need because on the Web there are too many sources of varying quality and too much information. Some information is valid, some outdated, some wrong, and most sources talk about obscure details. Anyone who is a newcomer and wishes to learn something about the Semantic Web, or who wishes to set up a course on the Semantic Web, is faced with these problems. This book is meant to help out.

A textbook must be selective in the topics it covers. Particularly in a field as fast developing as this, a textbook should concentrate on fundamental aspects that can reasonably be expected to remain relevant some time into the future. But, of course, authors always have their personal bias.

Even for the topics covered, this book is not meant to be a reference work that describes every small detail. Long books have already been written on certain topics, such as XML. And there is no need for a reference work in the Semantic Web area because all definitions and manuals are available online. Instead, we concentrate on the main ideas and techniques and provide enough detail to enable readers to engage with the material constructively and to build applications of their own.

This way readers will be equipped with sufficient knowledge to easily get the remaining details from other sources. In fact, an annotated list of references is found at the end of each chapter.

## Acknowledgments

We thank Jeen Broekstra, Michel Klein, and Marta Sabou for pioneering much of this material in our course on Web-based knowledge representation at the Free University in Amsterdam, and Annette ten Teije, Zharko Aleksovski and Wouter Jansweijer for critically reading early versions of the manuscript.

We thank Christoph Grimmer and Peter Koenig for proofreading parts of the book and assisting with the creation of the figures and with LaTeX processing.

Also, we wish to thank the MIT Press people for their professional assistance with the final preparation of the manuscript, and Christopher Manning for his LaTeX $2_\varepsilon$ macros.

# 1 *The Semantic Web Vision*

## 1.1 Today's Web

The World Wide Web has changed the way people communicate with each other and the way business is conducted. It lies at the heart of a revolution that is currently transforming the developed world toward a knowledge economy and, more broadly speaking, to a knowledge society.

This development has also changed the way we think of computers. Originally they were used for computing numerical calculations. Currently their predominant use is for information processing, typical applications being data bases, text processing, and games. At present there is a transition of focus towards the view of computers as entry points to the information highways.

Most of today's Web content is suitable for human consumption. Even Web content that is generated automatically from databases is usually presented without the original structural information found in databases. Typical uses of the Web today involve people's seeking and making use of information, searching for and getting in touch with other people, reviewing catalogs of online stores and ordering products by filling out forms, and viewing adult material.

These activities are not particularly well supported by software tools. Apart from the existence of links that establish connections between documents, the main valuable, indeed indispensable, tools are search engines.

Keyword-based search engines, such as AltaVista, Yahoo, and Google, are the main tools for using today's Web. It is clear that the Web would not have been the huge success it was, were it not for search engines. However, there are serious problems associated with their use:

- High recall, low precision. Even if the main relevant pages are retrieved, they are of little use if another 28,758 mildly relevant or irrelevant documents were also retrieved. Too much can easily become as bad as too little.

- Low or no recall. Often it happens that we don't get any answer for our request, or that important and relevant pages are not retrieved. Although low recall is a less frequent problem with current search engines, it does occur.

- Results are highly sensitive to vocabulary. Often our initial keywords do not get the results we want; in these cases the relevant documents use different terminology from the original query. This is unsatisfactory because semantically similar queries should return similar results.

- Results are single Web pages. If we need information that is spread over various documents, we must initiate several queries to collect the relevant documents, and then we must manually extract the partial information and put it together.

Interestingly, despite improvements in search engine technology, the difficulties remain essentially the same. It seems that the amount of Web content outpaces technological progress.

But even if a search is successful, it is the person who must browse selected documents to extract the information he is looking for. That is, there is not much support for retrieving the information, a very time-consuming activity. Therefore, the term *information retrieval*, used in association with search engines, is somewhat misleading; *location finder* might be a more appropriate term. Also, results of Web searches are not readily accessible by other software tools; search engines are often isolated applications.

The main obstacle to providing better support to Web users is that, at present, the meaning of Web content is not *machine-accessible*. Of course, there are tools that can retrieve texts, split them into parts, check the spelling, count their words. But when it comes to *interpreting* sentences and extracting useful information for users, the capabilities of current software are still very limited. It is simply difficult to distinguish the meaning of

I am a professor of computer science.

from

I am a professor of computer science, you may think. Well, . . .

Using text processing, how can the current situation be improved? One solution is to use the content as it is represented today and to develop increasingly sophisticated techniques based on artificial intelligence and computational linguistics. This approach has been followed for some time now, but despite some advances the task still appears too ambitious.

An alternative approach is to represent Web content in a form that is more easily machine-processable[1] and to use intelligent techniques to take advantage of these representations. We refer to this plan of revolutionizing the Web as the *Semantic Web* initiative. It is important to understand that the Semantic Web will not be a new global information highway parallel to the existing World Wide Web; instead it will gradually evolve out of the existing Web.

The Semantic Web is propagated by the World Wide Web Consortium (W3C), an international standardization body for the Web. The driving force of the Semantic Web initiative is Tim Berners-Lee, the very person who invented the WWW in the late 1980s. He expects from this initiative the realization of his original vision of the Web, a vision where the meaning of information played a far more important role than it does in today's Web.

The development of the Semantic Web has a lot of industry momentum, and governments are investing heavily. The U.S. government has established the DARPA Agent Markup Language (DAML) Project, and the Semantic Web is among the key action lines of the European Union's Sixth Framework Programme.

## 1.2  From Today's Web to the Semantic Web: Examples

### 1.2.1  Knowledge Management

Knowledge management concerns itself with acquiring, accessing, and maintaining knowledge within an organization. It has emerged as a key activity of large businesses because they view internal knowledge as an intellectual asset from which they can draw greater productivity, create new value, and increase their competitiveness. Knowledge management is particularly important for international organizations with geographically dispersed departments.

---

1. In the literature the term *machine understandable* is used quite often. We believe it is the wrong word because it gives the wrong impression. It is not necessary for intelligent agents to *understand* information; it is sufficient for them to process information effectively, which sometimes causes people to think the machine really understands.

Most information is currently available in a weakly structured form, for example, text, audio, and video. From the knowledge management perspective, the current technology suffers from limitations in the following areas:

- Searching information. Companies usually depend on keyword-based search engines, the limitations of which we have outlined.

- Extracting information. Human time and effort are required to browse the retrieved documents for relevant information. Current intelligent agents are unable to carry out this task in a satisfactory fashion.

- Maintaining information. Currently there are problems, such as inconsistencies in terminology and failure to remove outdated information.

- Uncovering information. New knowledge implicitly existing in corporate databases is extracted using data mining. However, this task is still difficult for distributed, weakly structured collections of documents.

- Viewing information. Often it is desirable to restrict access to certain information to certain groups of employees. "Views", which hide certain information, are known from the area of databases but are hard to realize over an intranet (or the Web).

The aim of the Semantic Web is to allow much more advanced knowledge management systems:

- Knowledge will be organized in conceptual spaces according to its meaning.

- Automated tools will support maintenance by checking for inconsistencies and extracting new knowledge.

- Keyword-based search will be replaced by query answering: requested knowledge will be retrieved, extracted, and presented in a human-friendly way.

- Query answering over several documents will be supported.

- Defining who may view certain parts of information (even parts of documents) will be possible.

## 1.2.2 Business-to-Consumer Electronic Commerce

Business-to-consumer (B2C) electronic commerce is the predominant commercial experience of Web users. A typical scenario involves a user's visiting one or several online shops, browsing their offers, selecting and ordering products.

Ideally, a user would collect information about prices, terms, and conditions (such as availability) of all, or at least all major, online shops and then proceed to select the best offer. But manual browsing is too time-consuming to be conducted on this scale. Typically a user will visit one or a very few online stores before making a decision.

To alleviate this situation, tools for shopping around on the Web are available in the form of shopbots, software agents that visit several shops, extract product and price information, and compile a market overview. Their functionality is provided by wrappers, programs that extract information from an online store. One wrapper per store must be developed. This approach suffers from several drawbacks.

The information is extracted from the online store site through keyword search and other means of textual analysis. This process makes use of assumptions about the proximity of certain pieces of information (for example, the price is indicated by the word *price* followed by the symbol $ followed by a positive number). This heuristic approach is error-prone; it is not always guaranteed to work. Because of these difficulties only limited information is extracted. For example, shipping expenses, delivery times, restrictions on the destination country, level of security, and privacy policies are typically not extracted. But all these factors may be significant for the user's decision making. In addition, programming wrappers is time-consuming, and changes in the online store outfit require costly reprogramming.

The Semantic Web will allow the development of software agents that can *interpret* the product information and the terms of service.

- Pricing and product information will be extracted correctly, and delivery and privacy policies will be interpreted and compared to the user requirements.

- Additional information about the reputation of online shops will be retrieved from other sources, for example, independent rating agencies or consumer bodies.

- The low-level programming of wrappers will become obsolete.

- More sophisticated shopping agents will be able to conduct automated negotiations, on the buyer's behalf, with shop agents.

### 1.2.3    Business-to-Business Electronic Commerce

Most users associate the commercial part of the Web with B2C e-commerce, but the greatest economic promise of all online technologies lies in the area of business-to-business (B2B) e-commerce.

Traditionally businesses have exchanged their data using the Electronic Data Interchange (EDI) approach. However this technology is complicated and understood only by experts. It is difficult to program and maintain, and it is error-prone. Each B2B communication requires separate programming, so such communications are costly. Finally, EDI is an isolated technology. The interchanged data cannot be easily integrated with other business applications.

The Internet appears to be an ideal infrastructure for business-to-business communication. Businesses have increasingly been looking at Internet-based solutions, and new business models such as *B2B portals* have emerged. Still, B2B e-commerce is hampered by the lack of standards. HTML (hypertext markup language) is too weak to support the outlined activities effectively: it provides neither the structure nor the semantics of information. The new standard of XML is a big improvement but can still support communications only in cases where there is a priori agreement on the vocabulary to be used and on its meaning.

The realization of the Semantic Web will allow businesses to enter partnerships without much overhead. Differences in terminology will be resolved using standard *abstract domain models*, and data will be interchanged using translation services. Auctioning, negotiations, and drafting contracts will be carried out automatically (or semiautomatically) by software agents.

### 1.2.4    Personal Agents: A Future Scenario

Michael had just had a minor car accident and was feeling some neck pain. His primary care physician suggested a series of physical therapy sessions. Michael asked his Semantic Web agent to work out some possibilities.

The agent retrieved details of the recommended therapy from the doctor's agent and looked up the list of therapists maintained by Michael's health insurance company. The agent checked for those located within a radius of 10 km from Michael's office or home, and looked up their reputation according to trusted rating services. Then it tried to match available appointment times with Michael's calendar. In a few minutes the agent returned two proposals. Unfortunately, Michael was not happy with either of them. One therapist had offered appointments in two weeks' time; for the other Michael would have to drive during rush hour. Therefore, Michael decided to set stricter time constraints and asked the agent to try again.

A few minutes later the agent came back with an alternative: A therapist with an excellent reputation who had available appointments starting in two days. However, there were a few minor problems. Some of Michael's less important work appointments would have to be rescheduled. The agent offered to make arrangements if this solution were adopted. Also, the therapist was not listed on the insurer's site because he charged more than the insurer's maximum coverage. The agent had found his name from an independent list of therapists and had already checked that Michael was entitled to the insurer's maximum coverage, according to the insurer's policy. It had also negotiated with the therapist's agent a special discount. The therapist had only recently decided to charge more than average and was keen to find new patients.

Michael was happy with the recommendation because he would have to pay only a few dollars extra. However, because he had installed the Semantic Web agent a few days ago, he asked it for explanations of some of its assertions: how was the therapist's reputation established, why was it necessary for Michael to reschedule some of his work appointments, how was the price negotiation conducted? The agent provided appropriate information.

Michael was satisfied. His new Semantic Web agent was going to make his busy life easier. He asked the agent to take all necessary steps to finalize the task.

## 1.3 Semantic Web Technologies

The scenarios outlined in section 1.2 are not science fiction; they do not require revolutionary scientific progress to be achieved. We can reasonably claim that the challenge is an engineering and technology adoption rather than a scientific one: partial solutions to all important parts of the problem exist. At present, the greatest needs are in the areas of integration, standardization, development of tools, and adoption by users. But, of course, further technological progress will lead to a more advanced Semantic Web than can, in principle, be achieved today.

In the following sections we outline a few technologies that are necessary for achieving the functionalities previously outlined.

### 1.3.1    Explicit Metadata

Currently, Web content is formatted for human readers rather than programs. HTML is the predominant language in which Web pages are written (directly or using tools). A portion of a typical Web page of a physical therapist might look like this:

```
<h1>Agilitas Physiotherapy Centre</h1>
Welcome to the home page of the Agilitas Physiotherapy Centre.
Do you feel pain? Have you had an injury? Let our staff
Lisa Davenport, Kelly Townsend (our lovely secretary)
and Steve Matthews take care of your body and soul.

<h2>Consultation hours</h2>
  Mon 11am - 7pm<br>
  Tue 11am - 7pm<br>
  Wed 3pm - 7pm<br>
  Thu 11am - 7pm<br>
  Fri 11am - 3pm<p>
  But note that we do not offer consultation
  during the weeks of the
  <a href=". . .">State Of Origin</a> games.
```

For people the information is presented in a satisfactory way, but machines will have their problems. Keyword-based searches will identify the words *physiotherapy* and *consultation hours*. And an intelligent agent might even be able to identify the personnel of the center. But it will have trouble distinguishing therapists from the secretary, and even more trouble with finding the exact consultation hours (for which it would have to follow the link to the State Of Origin games to find when they take place).

The Semantic Web approach to solving these problems is not the development of superintelligent agents. Instead it proposes to attack the problem from the Web page side. If HTML is replaced by more appropriate languages, then the Web pages could carry their content on their sleeve. In addition to containing formatting information aimed at producing a document for human readers, they could contain information about their content. In our example, there might be information such as

```
<company>
  <treatmentOffered>Physiotherapy</treatmentOffered>
  <companyName>Agilitas Physiotherapy Centre</companyName>
  <staff>
    <therapist>Lisa Davenport</therapist>
    <therapist>Steve Matthews</therapist>
    <secretary>Kelly Townsend</secretary>
  </staff>
</company>
```

This representation is far more easily processable by machines. The term *metadata* refers to such information: data about data. Metadata capture part of the *meaning* of data, thus the term *semantic* in Semantic Web.

In our example scenarios in section 1.2 there seemed to be no barriers in the access to information in Web pages: therapy details, calendars and appointments, prices and product descriptions, it seemed like all this information could be directly retrieved from existing Web content. But, as we explained, this will not happen using text-based manipulation of information but rather by taking advantage of machine-processable metadata.

As with the current development of Web pages, users will not have to be computer science experts to develop Web pages; they will be able to use tools for this purpose. Still, the question remains why users should care, why they should abandon HTML for Semantic Web languages. Perhaps we can give an optimist answer if we compare the situation today to the beginnings of the Web. The first users decided to adopt HTML because it had been adopted as a standard and they were expecting benefits from being early adopters. Others followed when more and better Web tools became available. And soon HTML was a universally accepted standard.

Similarly, we are currently observing the early adoption of XML. While not sufficient in itself for the realization of the Semantic Web vision, XML is an important first step. Early users, perhaps some large organizations interested in knowledge management and B2B e-commerce, will adopt *XML* and *RDF*, the current Semantic Web-related W3C standards. And the momentum will lead to more and more tool vendors' and end users' adopting the technology.

This will be a decisive step in the Semantic Web venture, but it is also a challenge. As we mentioned, the greatest current challenge is not scientific but rather one of technology adoption.

### 1.3.2   Ontologies

The term *ontology* originates from philosophy. In that context, it is used as
the name of a subfield of philosophy, namely, the study of the nature of ex-
istence (the literal translation of the Greek word $O \nu \tau o \lambda o \gamma i \alpha$), the branch of
metaphysics concerned with identifying, in the most general terms, the kinds
of things that actually exist, and how to describe them. For example, the observation that the world is made up of specific objects that can be grouped
into abstract classes based on shared properties is a typical ontological com-
mitment.

However, in more recent years, *ontology* has become one of the many
words hijacked by computer science and given a specific technical meaning
that is rather different from the original one. Instead of "ontology" we now
speak of *"an* ontology". For our purposes, we will uses T.R. Gruber's definition, later refined by R. Studer: *An ontology is an explicit and formal specification
of a conceptualization.*

In general, an ontology describes formally a domain of discourse. Typically, an ontology consists of a finite list of terms and the relationships between these terms. The *terms* denote important *concepts* (*classes* of objects) of
the domain. For example, in a university setting, staff members, students,
courses, lecture theaters, and disciplines are some important concepts.

The *relationships* typically include hierarchies of classes. A hierarchy specifies a class $C$ to be a subclass of another class $C'$ if every object in $C$ is also
included in $C'$. For example, all faculty are staff members. Figure 1.1 shows
a hierarchy for the university domain.

Apart from subclass relationships, ontologies may include information
such as

- properties (X teaches Y)

- value restrictions (only faculty members can teach courses)

- disjointness statements (faculty and general staff are disjoint)

- specification of logical relationships between objects (every department
  must include at least ten faculty members)

In the context of the Web, ontologies provide *a shared understanding of a domain*. Such a shared understanding is necessary to overcome differences in
terminology. One application's zip code may be the same as another application's area code. Another problem is that two applications may use the same

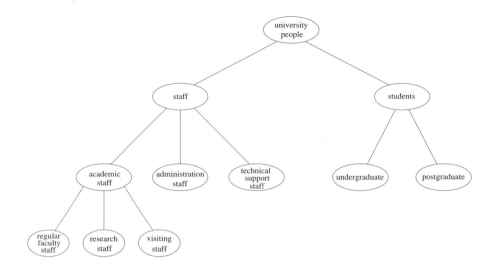

**Figure 1.1**   A hierarchy

term with different meanings. In university A, a course may refer to a degree (like computer science), while in university B it may mean a single subject (CS 101). Such differences can be overcome by mapping the particular terminology to a shared ontology or by defining direct mappings between the ontologies. In either case, it is easy to see that ontologies support semantic interoperability .

Ontologies are useful for the organization and navigation of Web sites. Many Web sites today expose on the left-hand side of the page the top levels of a concept hierarchy of terms. The user may click on one of them to expand the subcategories.

Also, ontologies are useful for improving the accuracy of Web searches. The search engines can look for pages that refer to a precise *concept* in an ontology instead of collecting all pages in which certain, generally ambiguous, keywords occur. In this way, differences in terminology between Web pages and the queries can be overcome.

In addition, Web searches can exploit generalization/specialization information. If a query fails to find any relevant documents, the search engine may suggest to the user a more general query. It is even conceivable for the engine to run such queries proactively to reduce the reaction time in case the user adopts a suggestion. Or if too many answers are retrieved, the search engine may suggest to the user some specializations.

In Artificial Intelligence (AI) there is a long tradition of developing and using ontology languages. It is a foundation Semantic Web research can build upon. At present, the most important ontology languages for the Web are the following:

- XML provides a surface syntax for structured documents but imposes no semantic constraints on the meaning of these documents.

- XML Schema is a language for restricting the structure of XML documents.

- RDF is a data model for objects ("resources") and relations between them; it provides a simple semantics for this data model; and these data models can be represented in an XML syntax.

- RDF Schema is a vocabulary description language for describing properties and classes of RDF resources, with a semantics for generalization hierarchies of such properties and classes.

- OWL is a richer vocabulary description language for describing properties and classes, such as relations between classes (e.g., disjointness), cardinality (e.g. "exactly one"), equality, richer typing of properties, characteristics of properties (e.g., symmetry), and enumerated classes.

### 1.3.3    Logic

Logic is the discipline that studies the principles of reasoning; it goes back to Aristotle. In general, logic offers, first, *formal languages* for expressing knowledge. Second, logic provides us with *well-understood formal semantics*: in most logics, the meaning of sentences is defined without the need to operationalize the knowledge. Often we speak of declarative knowledge: we describe *what* holds without caring about *how* it can be deduced.

And third, automated reasoners can deduce (infer) conclusions from the given knowledge, thus making implicit knowledge explicit. Such reasoners have been studied extensively in AI. Here is an example of an inference. Suppose we know that all professors are faculty members, that all faculty members are staff members, and that Michael is a professor. In predicate logic the information is expressed as follows:

$$prof(X) \rightarrow faculty(X)$$
$$faculty(X) \rightarrow staff(X)$$
$$prof(michael)$$

Then we can deduce the following:

$$faculty(michael)$$
$$staff(michael)$$
$$prof(X) \rightarrow staff(X)$$

Note that this example involves knowledge typically found in ontologies. Thus logic can be used to uncover ontological knowledge that is implicitly given. By doing so, it can also help uncover unexpected relationships and inconsistencies.

But logic is more general than ontologies. It can also be used by intelligent agents for making decisions and selecting courses of action. For example, a shop agent may decide to grant a discount to a customer based on the rule

$$loyalCustomer(X) \rightarrow discount(5\%)$$

where the loyalty of customers is determined from data stored in the corporate database. Generally there is a trade-off between expressive power and computational efficiency. The more expressive a logic is, the more computationally expensive it becomes to draw conclusions. And drawing certain conclusions may become impossible if noncomputability barriers are encountered. Luckily, most knowledge relevant to the Semantic Web seems to be of a relatively restricted form. For example, our previous examples involved *rules* of the form, "If conditions, then conclusion," and only finitely many objects needed to be considered. This subset of logic is tractable and is supported by efficient reasoning tools.

An important advantage of logic is that it can provide *explanations* for conclusions: the series of inference steps can be retraced. Moreover AI researchers have developed ways of presenting an explanation in a human-friendly way, by organizing a proof as a natural deduction and by grouping a number of low-level inference steps into metasteps that a person will typically consider a single proof step. Ultimately an explanation will trace an answer back to a given set of facts and the inference rules used.

Explanations are important for the Semantic Web because they increase users' confidence in Semantic Web agents (see the physiotherapy example in section 1.2.4). Tim Berners-Lee speaks of an "Oh yeah?" button that would ask for an explanation.

Explanations will also be necessary for activities between agents. While some agents will be able to draw logical conclusions, others will only have the capability to *validate proofs*, that is, to check whether a claim made by another agent is substantiated. Here is a simple example. Suppose agent 1, representing an online shop, sends a message "You owe me $80" (not in natural language, of course, but in a formal, machine-processable language) to agent 2, representing a person. Then agent 2 might ask for an explanation, and agent 1 might respond with a sequence of the form

Web log of a purchase over $80

Proof of delivery (for example, tracking number of UPS)

Rule from the shop's terms and conditions:

$$purchase(X, Item) \land price(Item, Price) \land delivered(Item, X)$$
$$\rightarrow owes(X, Price)$$

Thus facts will typically be traced to some Web addresses (the trust of which will be verifiable by agents), and the rules may be a part of a shared commerce ontology or the policy of the online shop.

For logic to be useful on the Web it must be usable in conjunction with other data, and it must be machine-processable as well. Therefore, there is ongoing work on representing logical knowledge and proofs in Web languages. Initial approaches work at the level of XML, but in the future rules and proofs will need to be represented at the level of RDF and ontology languages, such as DAML+OIL and OWL.

### 1.3.4   Agents

Agents are pieces of software that work autonomously and proactively. Conceptually they evolved out of the concepts of object-oriented programming and component-based software development.

A personal agent on the Semantic Web (figure 1.2) will receive some tasks and preferences from the person, seek information from Web sources, communicate with other agents, compare information about user requirements and preferences, select certain choices, and give answers to the user. An example of such an agent is Michael's private agent in the physiotherapy example of section 1.2.4.

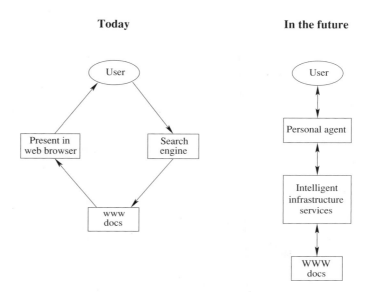

**Figure 1.2**   Intelligent personal agents

It should be noted that agents will not replace human users on the Semantic Web, nor will they necessarily make decisions. In many, if not most, cases their role will be to collect and organize information, and present choices for the users to select from, as Michael's personal agent did in offering a selection between the two best solutions it could find, or as a travel agent does that looks for travel offers to fit a person's given preferences.

Semantic Web agents will make use of all the technologies we have outlined:

- Metadata will be used to identify and extract information from Web sources.

- Ontologies will be used to assist in Web searches, to interpret retrieved information, and to communicate with other agents.

- Logic will be used for processing retrieved information and for drawing conclusions.

Further technologies will also be needed, such as agent communication languages. Also, for advanced applications it will be useful to represent formally the beliefs, desires, and intentions of agents, and to create and maintain user models. However, these points are somewhat orthogonal to the Semantic Web technologies. Therefore they are not discussed further in this book.

### 1.3.5   The Semantic Web versus Artificial Intelligence

As we have said, most of the technologies needed for the realization of the Semantic Web build upon work in the area of artificial intelligence. Given that AI has a long history, not always commercially successful, one might worry that, in the worst case, the Semantic Web will repeat AI's errors: big promises that raise too high expectations, which turn out not to be fulfilled (at least not in the promised time frame).

This worry is unjustified. The realization of the Semantic Web vision does not rely on human-level intelligence; in fact, as we have tried to explain, the challenges are approached in a different way. The full problem of AI is a deep scientific one, perhaps comparable to the central problems of physics (explain the physical world) or biology (explain the living world). So seen, the difficulties in achieving human-level Artificial Intelligence within ten or twenty years, as promised at some points in the past, should not have come as a surprise.

But on the Semantic Web partial solutions will work. Even if an intelligent agent is not able to come to all conclusions that a human user might draw, the agent will still contribute to a Web much superior to the current Web. This brings us to another difference. If the ultimate goal of AI is to build an intelligent agent exhibiting human-level intelligence (and higher), the goal of the Semantic Web is to assist human users in their day-to-day online activities.

It is clear that the Semantic Web will make extensive use of current AI technology and that advances in that technology will lead to a better Semantic Web. But there is no need to wait until AI reaches a higher level of achievement; current AI technology is already sufficient to go a long way toward realizing the Semantic Web vision.

## 1.4   A Layered Approach

The development of the Semantic Web proceeds in steps, each step building a *layer* on top of another. The pragmatic justification for this approach is that it is easier to achieve consensus on small steps, whereas it is much harder to get everyone on board if too much is attempted. Usually there are several research groups moving in different directions; this competition of ideas is a major driving force for scientific progress. However, from an engineering perspective there is a need to standardize. So, if most researchers agree on certain issues and disagree on others, it makes sense to fix the points of agreement. This way, even if the more ambitious research efforts should fail, there will be at least partial positive outcomes.

Once a standard has been established, many more groups and companies will adopt it, instead of waiting to see which of the alternative research lines will be successful in the end. The nature of the Semantic Web is such that companies and single users must build tools, add content, and use that content. We cannot wait until the full Semantic Web vision materializes — it may take another ten years for it to be realized to its full extent (as envisioned today, of course).

In building one layer of the Semantic Web on top of another, two principles should be followed:

- Downward compatibility. Agents fully aware of a layer should also be able to interpret and use information written at lower levels. For example, agents aware of the semantics of OWL can take full advantage of information written in RDF and RDF Schema.

- Upward partial understanding. On the other hand, agents fully aware of a layer should take at least partial advantage of information at higher levels. For example, an agent aware only of the RDF and RDF Schema semantics can interpret knowledge written in OWL partly, by disregarding those elements that go beyond RDF and RDF Schema.

Figure 1.3 shows the "layer cake" of the Semantic Web (due to Tim Berners-Lee), which describes the main layers of the Semantic Web design and vision.

At the bottom we find *XML*, a language that lets one write structured Web documents with a user-defined vocabulary. XML is particularly suitable for sending documents across the Web.

*RDF* is a basic data model, like the entity-relationship model, for writing simple statements about Web objects (resources). The RDF data model does not rely on XML, but RDF has an XML-based syntax. Therefore, in figure 1.3, it is located on top of the XML layer.

*RDF Schema* provides modeling primitives for organizing Web objects into hierarchies. Key primitives are classes and properties, subclass and subproperty relationships, and domain and range restrictions. RDF Schema is based on RDF.

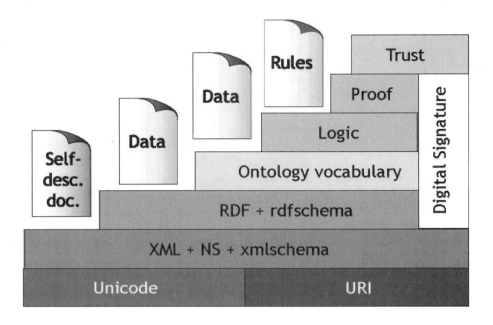

**Figure 1.3**   A layered approach to the Semantic Web

RDF Schema can be viewed as a primitive language for writing ontologies. But there is a need for more powerful *ontology languages* that expand RDF Schema and allow the representations of more complex relationships between Web objects. The *Logic* layer is used to enhance the ontology language further and to allow the writing of application-specific declarative knowledge.

The *Proof layer* involves the actual deductive process as well as the representation of proofs in Web languages (from lower levels) and proof validation.

Finally, the *Trust layer* will emerge through the use of *digital signatures* and other kinds of knowledge, based on recommendations by trusted agents or on rating and certification agencies and consumer bodies. Sometimes "Web of Trust" is used to indicate that trust will be organized in the same distributed and chaotic way as the WWW itself. Being located at the top of the pyramid, trust is a high-level and crucial concept: the Web will only achieve its full potential when users have trust in its operations (security) and in the quality of information provided.

## 1.5    Book Overview

In this book we concentrate on the Semantic Web technologies that have reached a reasonable degree of maturity.

In Chapter 2 we discuss XML and related technologies. XML introduces structure to Web documents, thus supporting syntactic interoperability. The structure of a document can be made machine-accessible through DTDs and XML Schema. We also discuss namespaces; accessing and querying XML documents using XPath; and transforming XML documents with XSLT.

In Chapter 3 we discuss RDF and RDF Schema. RDF is a language in which we can express statements about objects (resources); it is a standard data model for machine-processable semantics. RDF Schema offers a number of modeling primitives for organizing RDF vocabularies in typed hierarchies.

Chapter 4 discusses OWL, the current proposal for a Web ontology language. It offers more modeling primitives, compared to RDF Schema, and has a clean, formal semantics.

Chapter 5 is devoted to rules, both monotonic and nonmonotonic, in the framework of the Semantic Web. While this layer has not yet been fully defined, the principles to be adopted are quite clear, so it makes sense to present them.

Chapter 6 discusses several application domains and explains the benefits that they will draw from the materialization of the Semantic Web vision.

Chapter 7 describes the development of ontology-based systems for the Web and contains a miniproject that employs much of the technology described in this book.

Finally, chapter 8 discusses briefly a few issues which are currently under debate in the Semantic Web community.

## 1.6    Summary

- The Semantic Web is an initiative that aims at improving the current state of the World Wide Web.

- The key idea is the use of machine-processable Web information.

- Key technologies include explicit metadata, ontologies, logic and inferencing, and intelligent agents.

- The development of the Semantic Web proceeds in layers.

## Suggested Reading

An excellent introductory article, from which, among others, the scenario in section 1.2.4 was adapted.

- T. Berners-Lee, J. Hendler, and O. Lassila. The Semantic Web. *Scientific American* 284 (May 2001): 34-43.

An inspirational book about the history (and the future) of the Web is

- T. Berners-Lee, with M. Fischetti. *Weaving the Web*. San Francisco: Harper, 1999.

Many introductory articles on the Semantic Web are available online. Here we list a few:

- T. Berners-Lee. Semantic Web Road Map. September 1998.
  <http://www.w3.org/DesignIssues/Semantic.html>.

- T. Berners-Lee. Evolvability. March 1998.
  <http://www.w3.org/DesignIssues/Evolution.html>.

- T. Berners-Lee. What the Semantic Web Can Represent. September 1998.
  <http://www.w3.org/DesignIssues/RDFnot.html>.

- E. Dumbill. The Semantic Web: A Primer. November 1, 2000.
  <http://www.xml.com/pub/a/2000/11/01/semanticweb/>.

- F. van Harmelen and D. Fensel. Practical Knowledge Representation for the Web. <http://www.cs.vu.nl/~frankh/postscript/IJCAI99-III.html>.

- J. Hendler. Agents and the Semantic Web. *IEEE Intelligent Systems* 16 (March-April 2001): 30-37.
  Preprint at <http://www.cs.umd.edu/users/hendler/AgentWeb.html>.

- S. Palmer. The Semantic Web, Taking Form.
  <http://infomesh.net/2001/06/swform/>.

- S. Palmer. The Semantic Web: An Introduction.
  <http://infomesh.net/2001/Swintro/>.

- A. Swartz. The Semantic Web in Breadth.
  <http://logicerror.com/semanticWeb-long>.

- A. Swartz and J. Hendler. The Semantic Web: A Network of Content for the Digital City. <http://blogspace.com/rdf/SwartzHendler.html>.

- R. Jasper and A. Tyler. The Role of Semantics and Inference in the Semantic Web: A Commercial Challenge.
  <http://www.semanticweb.org/SWWS/program/position/soi-jasper.pdf>.

There are several courses on the Semantic Web that have extensive material online:

- F. van Harmelen et al. Web-Based Knowledge Representation. <http://www.cs.vu.nl/~marta/wbkr.html>.

- J. Heflin. The Semantic Web. <http://www.cse.lehigh.edu/~heflin/courses/semweb/>.

- A. Sheth. Semantic Web. <http://lsdis.cs.uga.edu/SemWebCourse/index.html>.

- H. Boley, S. Decker, and M. Sintek. Tutorial on Knowledge Markup Techniques. <http://www.dfki.uni-kl.de/km/knowmark/>.

A number of Web sites maintain up-to-date information about the Semantic Web and related topics:

- <http://www.SemanticWeb.org>.

- <http://www.w3.org/2001/sw/>.

- <http://www.ontology.org>.

There is a good selection of research papers providing technical information on issues relating to the Semantic Web:

- D. Fensel, J. Hendler, H. Lieberman and W. Wahlster, eds. *Spinning the Semantic Web*. Cambridge, MA: MIT Press, 2003.

- J. Davies, D. Fensel and F. van Harmelen, eds. *Towards the Semantic Web: Ontology-Driven Knowledge Management*. New York: Wiley, 2002.

- The conference series of the *International Semantic Web Conference* (see <http://www.semanticweb.org/>).

# 2 *Structured Web Documents in XML*

## 2.1 Introduction

Today HTML (hypertext markup language) is the standard language in which Web pages are written. HTML, in turn, was derived from SGML (standard generalized markup language), an international standard (ISO 8879) for the definition of device- and system-independent methods of representing information, both human- and machine-readable. Such standards are important because they enable effective communication, thus supporting technological progress and business collaboration. In the WWW area, standards are set by the W3C (World Wide Web Consortium); they are called *recommendations*, in acknowledgment of the fact that in a distributed environment without central authority, standards cannot be enforced.

Languages conforming to SGML are called SGML applications. HTML is such an application; it was developed because SGML was considered far too complex for Internet-related purposes. XML (extensible markup language) is another SGML application, and its development was driven by shortcomings of HTML. We can work out some of the motivations for XML by considering a simple example, a Web page that contains information about a particular book.

```
<h2>Nonmonotonic Reasoning:  Context-Dependent
    Reasoning</h2>
<i>by <b>V. Marek</b> and <b>M. Truszczynski</b></i><br>
Springer 1993<br>
ISBN 0387976892
```

A typical XML representation of the the same information might look like this:

```
<book>
  <title>
    Nonmonotonic Reasoning:   Context-Dependent Reasoning
  </title>
  <author>V. Marek</author>
  <author>M. Truszczynski</author>
  <publisher>Springer</publisher>
  <year>1993</year>
  <ISBN>0387976892</ISBN>
</book>
```

Before we turn to differences between the HTML and XML representations, let us observe a few similarities. First, both representations use *tags*, such as <h2> and </year>. Indeed both HTML and XML are *markup languages*: they allow one to write some content and provide information about what role that content plays.

Like HTML, XML is based on tags. These tags may be nested (tags within tags). All tags in XML must be closed (for example, for an opening tag <title> there must be a closing tag </title>), whereas in HTML some tags, such as <br>, may be left open. The enclosed content, together with its opening and closing tags, is referred to as an *element*. (The recent development of XHTML has brought HTML more in line with XML: any valid XHTML document is also a valid XML document, and as a consequence, opening and closing tags in XHTML are balanced).

A less formal observation is that human userss can read both HTML and XML representations quite easily. Both languages were designed to be easily understandable and usable by humans. But how about machines? Imagine an intelligent agent trying to retrieve the names of the authors of the book in the previous example. Suppose the HTML page could be located with a Web search (something that is not at all clear; the limitations of current search engines are well documented). There is no *explicit* information as to who the authors are. A reasonable guess would be that the authors' names appear immediately after the title or immediately follow the word *by*. But there is no guarantee that these conventions are always followed. And even if they were, are there two authors, "V. Marek" and "M. Truszczynski", or just one, called "V. Marek and M. Truszczynski"? Clearly, more text processing is needed to answer this question, processing that is open to errors.

The problems arise from the fact that the HTML document does not contain structural information, that is, information about pieces of the document and their relationships. In contrast, the XML document is far more easily accessible to machines because every piece of information is described. Moreover, their *relations* are also defined through the nesting structure. For example, the <author> tags appear within the <book> tags, so they describe properties of the particular book. A machine processing the XML document would be able to deduce that the author element refers to the enclosing book element, rather than having to infer this fact from proximity considerations, as in HTML. An additional advantage is that XML allows the definition of constraints on values (for example, that a year must be a number of four digits, that the number must be less than 3,000). *XML allows the representation of information that is also machine-accessible.*

Of course, we must admit that the HTML representation provides more than the XML representation: the formatting of the document is also described. However, this feature is not a strength but a weakness of HTML: it *must* specify the formatting; in fact, the main use of an HTML document is to display information (apart from linking to other documents). On the other hand, *XML separates content from formatting.* The same information can be displayed in different ways, without requiring multiple copies of the same content; moreover, the content may be used for purposes other than display.

Let us now consider another example, a famous law of physics. Consider the HTML text

```
<h2>Relationship force-mass</h2>
<i>F = M × a</i>
```

and the XML representation

```
<equation>
  <meaning>Relationship force-mass</meaning>
  <leftside>F</leftside>
  <rightside>M × a</rightside>
</equation>
```

If we compare the HTML document to the previous HTML document, we notice that both use basically the same tags. That is not surprising, since they are *predefined*. In contrast, the second XML document uses completely different tags from the first XML document. This observation is related to the intended use of representations. HTML representations are intended to display information, so the set of tags is fixed: lists, bold, color, and so on. In XML we may use information in various ways, and it is up to the user to define a vocabulary suitable for the application. Therefore, *XML is a metalanguage for markup: it does not have a fixed set of tags but allows users to define tags of their own.*

Just as people cannot communicate effectively if they don't use a common language, applications on the WWW must agree on common vocabularies if they need to communicate and collaborate. Communities and business sectors are in the process of defining their specialized vocabularies, creating XML applications (or extensions; thus the term *extensible* in the name of XML). Such XML applications have been defined in various domains, for example, mathematics (MathML), bioinformatics (BSML), human resources (HRML), astronomy (AML), news (NewsML), and investment (IRML).

Also, the W3C has defined various languages on top of XML, such as SVG and SMIL. This approach has also been taken for RDF (see chapter 3).

It should be noted that XML can serve as a *uniform data exchange format* between applications. In fact, XML's use as a data exchange format between applications nowadays far outstrips its originally intended use as document markup language. Companies often need to retrieve information from their customers and business partners, and update their corporate databases accordingly. If there is not an agreed common standard like XML, then specialized processing and querying software must be developed for each partner separately, leading to technical overhead; moreover, the software must be updated every time a partner decides to change its own database format.

In this chapter, section 2.2 describes the XML language in more detail, and section 2.3 describes the structuring of XML documents. In relational databases, the structure of tables must be defined. Similarly, the structure of an XML document must be defined. This can be done by writing a DTD (document data definition), the older approach, or an XML schema, the modern approach that will gradually replace DTDs.

Section 2.4 describes namespaces, which support the modularization of DTDs and XML schemas. Section 2.5 is devoted to the accessing and querying of XML documents, using XPath. Finally, section 2.6 shows how XML documents can be transformed to be displayed (or for other purposes), using XSL and XSLT.

## 2.2 The XML Language

An *XML document* consists of a prolog, a number of elements, and an optional epilog (not discussed here).

### 2.2.1 Prolog

The prolog consists of an XML declaration and an optional reference to external structuring documents. Here is an example of an *XML declaration*:

```
<?xml version="1.0" encoding="UTF-16"?>
```

It specifies that the current document is an XML document, and defines the version and the character encoding used in the particular system (such as UTF-8, UTF-16, and ISO 8859-1). The character encoding is not mandatory, but its specification is considered good practice. Sometimes we also specify whether the document is self-contained, that is, whether it does not refer to external structuring documents:

```
<?xml version="1.0" encoding="UTF-16" standalone="no" ?>
```

A reference to external structuring documents looks like this:

```
<!DOCTYPE book SYSTEM "book.dtd">
```

Here the structuring information is found in a local file called book.dtd. Instead, the reference might be a URL. If only a locally recognized name or only a URL is used, then the label SYSTEM is used. If, however, one wishes to give both a local name and a URL, then the label PUBLIC should be used instead.

### 2.2.2 Elements

XML elements represent the "things" the XML document talks about, such as books, authors, and publishers. They compose the main concept of XML documents. An element consists of an *opening tag*, its *content*, and a *closing tag*. For example,

```
<lecturer>David Billington</lecturer>
```

Tag names can be chosen almost freely; there are very few restrictions. The most important ones are that the first character must be a letter, an underscore, or a colon; and that no name may begin with the string "xml" in any combination of cases (such as "Xml" and "xML").

The content may be text, or other elements, or nothing. For example,

```
<lecturer>
  <name>David Billington</name>
  <phone>+61-7-3875 507</phone>
</lecturer>
```

If there is no content, then the element is called *empty*. An empty element like

```
<lecturer></lecturer>
```

can be abbreviated as

```
<lecturer/>
```

### 2.2.3   Attributes

An empty element is not necessarily meaningless, because it may have some properties in terms of *attributes*. An attribute is a name-value pair inside the opening tag of an element:

```
<lecturer name="David Billington" phone="+61-7-3875 507"/>
```

Here is an example of attributes for a nonempty element:

```
<order orderNo="23456" customer="John Smith"
       date="October 15, 2002">
  <item itemNo="a528" quantity="1"/>
  <item itemNo="c817" quantity="3"/>
</order>
```

The same information could have been written as follows, replacing attributes by nested elements:

```
<order>
  <orderNo>23456</orderNo>
  <customer>John Smith</customer>
  <date>October 15, 2002</date>
  <item>
    <itemNo>a528</itemNo>
    <quantity>1</quantity>
  </item>
```

```
<item>
  <itemNo>c817</itemNo>
  <quantity>3</quantity>
</item>
</order>
```

When to use elements and when attributes is often a matter of taste. However, note that attributes cannot be nested.

### 2.2.4   Comments

A comment is a piece of text that is to be ignored by the parser. It has the form

```
<!-- This is a comment -->
```

### 2.2.5   Processing Instructions (PIs)

PIs provide a mechanism for passing information to an application about how to handle elements. The general form is

```
<?target instruction ?>
```

For example,

```
<?stylesheet type="text/css" href="mystyle.css"?>
```

PIs offer procedural possibilities in an otherwise declarative environment.

### 2.2.6   Well-Formed XML Documents

An XML document is well-formed if it is syntactically correct. Some syntactic rules are

- There is only one outermost element in the document (called the *root element*).

- Each element contains an opening and a corresponding closing tag.

- Tags may not overlap, as in
  `<author><name>Lee Hong</author></name>`.

- Attributes within an element have unique names.

- Element and tag names must be permissible.

### 2.2.7    The Tree Model of XML Documents

It is possible to represent well-formed XML documents as trees; thus trees provide a formal data model for XML. This representation is often instructive. As an example, consider the following document:

```
<?xml version="1.0" encoding="UTF-16"?>
<!DOCTYPE email SYSTEM "email.dtd">
<email>
  <head>
    <from name="Michael Maher"
          address="michaelmaher@cs.gu.edu.au"/>
    <to   name="Grigoris Antoniou"
          address="grigoris@cs.unibremen.de"/>
    <subject>Where is your draft?</subject>
  </head>
  <body>
  Grigoris, where is the draft of the paper
  you promised me last week?
  </body>
</email>
```

Figure 2.1 shows the tree representation of this XML document. It is an ordered labeled tree:

- There is exactly one root.

- There are no cycles.

- Each node, other than the root, has exactly one parent.

- Each node has a label.

- The order of elements is important.

However, whereas the order of elements is important, the order of attributes is not. So, the following two elements are equivalent:

```
<person lastname="Woo" firstname="Jason"/>
<person firstname="Jason" lastname="Woo"/>
```

This aspect is not represented properly in the tree. In general, we would require a more refined tree concept; for example, we should also differentiate between the different types of nodes (element node, attribute node etc.).

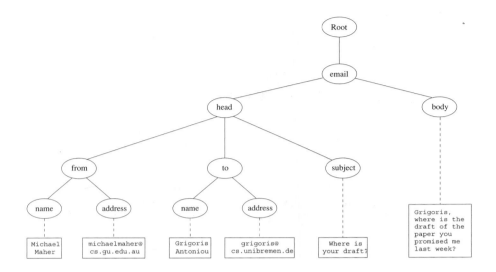

**Figure 2.1** Tree representation of an XML document

However, here we use graphs as illustrations, so we do not go into further detail.

Figure 2.1 also shows the difference between the *root* (representing the XML document), and the *root element*, in our case the `email` element. This distinction will play a role when we discuss addressing and querying XML documents in section 2.5.

## 2.3 Structuring

An XML document is well-formed if it respects certain syntactic rules. However, those rules say nothing specific about the structure of the document. Now, imagine two applications that try to communicate, and that they wish to use the same vocabulary. For this purpose it is necessary to define all the element and attribute names that may be used. Moreover, the structure should also be defined: what values an attribute may take, which elements may or must occur within other elements, and so on.

In the presence of such structuring information we have an enhanced possibility of document validation. We say that an XML document is *valid* if it is well-formed, uses structuring information, and respects that structuring information.

There are two ways of defining the structure of XML documents: DTDs, the older and more restricted way, and XML Schema, which offers extended possibilities, mainly for the definition of data types.

### 2.3.1    DTDs

**External and Internal DTDs**

The components of a DTD can be defined in a separate file (*external DTD*) or within the XML document itself (*internal DTD*). Usually it is better to use external DTDs, because their definitions can be used across several documents; otherwise duplication is inevitable, and the maintenance of consistency over time becomes difficult.

**Elements**

Consider the element

```
<lecturer>
  <name>David Billington</name>
  <phone>+61-7-3875 507</phone>
</lecturer>
```

from the previous section. A DTD for this element type[1] looks like this:

```
<!ELEMENT lecturer (name,phone)>
<!ELEMENT name (#PCDATA)>
<!ELEMENT phone (#PCDATA)>
```

The meaning of this DTD is as follows:

- The element types `lecturer`, `name`, and `phone` may be used in the document.

- A `lecturer` element contains a `name` element and a `phone` element, in that order.

---

1. The distinction between the element type `lecturer` and a particular element of this type, such as `David Billington`, should be clear. All particular elements of type `lecturer` (referred to as `lecturer` elements) share the same structure, which is defined here.

- A name element and a phone element may have any content. In DTDs, #PCDATA is the only atomic type for elements.

We express that a lecturer element contains either a name element or a phone element as follows:

```
<!ELEMENT lecturer (name|phone)>
```

It gets more difficult when we wish to specify that a lecturer element contains a name element and a phone element *in any order*. We can only use the trick

```
<!ELEMENT lecturer ((name,phone)|(phone,name))>
```

However, this approach suffers from practical limitations (imagine ten elements in any order).

**Attributes**

Consider the element

```
<order orderNo="23456" customer="John Smith"
       date="October 15, 2002">
  <item itemNo="a528" quantity="1"/>
  <item itemNo="c817" quantity="3"/>
</order>
```

from the previous section. A DTD for it looks like this:

```
<!ELEMENT order (item+)>
<!ATTLIST order
  orderNo   ID      #REQUIRED
  customer  CDATA   #REQUIRED
  date      CDATA   #REQUIRED>
<!ELEMENT item EMPTY>
<!ATTLIST item
  itemNo    ID      #REQUIRED
  quantity  CDATA   #REQUIRED
  comments  CDATA   #IMPLIED>
```

Compared to the previous example, a new aspect is that the item element type is defined to be empty. Another new aspect is the appearance of + after item in the definition of the order element type. It is one of the *cardinality operators*:

?:  appears zero times or once

\*:  appears zero or more times

+:  appears one or more times

No cardinality operator means exactly once.

In addition to defining elements, we have to define attributes. This is done in an *attribute list*. The first component is the name of the element type to which the list applies, followed by a list of triplets of attribute name, attribute type, and value type. An *attribute* name is a name that may be used in an XML document using a DTD.

### Attribute Types

They are similar to predefined data types, but the selection is very limited. The most important types are

- CDATA, a string (sequence of characters)

- ID, a name that is unique across the entire XML document

- IDREF, a reference to another element with an ID attribute carrying the same value as the IDREF attribute

- IDREFS, a series of IDREFs

- $(v_1| \ldots |v_n)$, an enumeration of all possible values

The selection is not satisfactory. For example, dates and numbers cannot be specified; they have to be interpreted as strings (CDATA); thus their specific structure cannot be enforced.

### Value Types

There are four value types:

- #REQUIRED. The attribute must appear in every occurrence of the element type in the XML document. In the previous example, itemNo and quantity must always appear within an item element.

- #IMPLIED. The appearance of the attribute is optional. In the example, comments are optional.

- #FIXED "value". Every element must have this attribute, which has always the value given after #FIXED in the DTD. A value given in an XML document is meaningless because it is overridden by the fixed value.

- "value". This specifies the default value for the attribute. If a specific value appears in the XML document, it overrides the default value. For example, the default encoding of the e-mail system may be "mime", but "binhex" will be used if specified explicitly by the user.

**Referencing**

Here is an example for the use of IDREF and IDREFS. First we give a DTD:

```
<!ELEMENT family (person*)>
<!ELEMENT person (name)>
<!ELEMENT name (#PCDATA)>
<!ATTLIST person
  id       ID     #REQUIRED
  mother   IDREF  #IMPLIED
  father   IDREF  #IMPLIED
  children IDREFS #IMPLIED>
```

An XML element that respects this DTD is the following:

```
<family>

  <person id="bob" mother="mary" father="peter">
    <name>Bob Marley</name>
  </person>

  <person id="bridget" mother="mary">
    <name>Bridget Jones</name>
  </person>

  <person id="mary" children="bob bridget">
    <name>Mary Poppins</name>
  </person>

  <person id="peter" children="bob">
    <name>Peter Marley</name>
  </person>

</family>
```

Readers should study the references between persons.

**A Concluding Example**

As a final example we give a DTD for the `email` element from the section 2.2.7:

```
<!ELEMENT email (head,body)>
<!ELEMENT head (from,to+,cc*,subject)>
<!ELEMENT from EMPTY>
<!ATTLIST from
   name      CDATA      #IMPLIED
   address   CDATA      #REQUIRED>
<!ELEMENT to EMPTY>
<!ATTLIST to
   name      CDATA      #IMPLIED
   address   CDATA      #REQUIRED>
<!ELEMENT cc EMPTY>
<!ATTLIST cc
   name      CDATA      #IMPLIED
   address   CDATA      #REQUIRED>
<!ELEMENT subject (#PCDATA)>
<!ELEMENT body (text,attachment*)>
<!ELEMENT text (#PCDATA)>
<!ELEMENT attachment EMPTY>
<!ATTLIST attachment
   encoding (mime|binhex) "mime"
   file      CDATA      #REQUIRED>
```

We go through some interesting parts of this DTD:

- A `head` element contains a `from` element, at least one `to` element, zero or more `cc` elements, and a `subject` element, in that order.

- In `from`, `to`, and `cc` elements the `name` attribute is not required; the `address` attribute on the other hand is always required.

- A `body` element contains a `text` element, possibly followed by a number of `attachment` elements.

- The `encoding` attribute of an `attachment` element must have either the value "`mime`" or "`binhex`", the former being the default value.

We conclude with two more remarks on DTDs. Firstly, a DTD can be interpreted as an Extended Backus-Naur Form (EBNF). For example, the declaration

```
<!ELEMENT email (head,body)>
```

is equivalent to the rule

```
email ::= head body
```

which means that an e-mail consists of a head followed by a body. And second, recursive definitions are possible in DTDs. For example,

```
<!ELEMENT bintree ((bintree root bintree)|emptytree)>
```

defines binary trees: a binary tree is the empty tree, or consists of a left subtree, a root, and a right subtree.

### 2.3.2 XML Schema

XML Schema offers a significantly richer language for defining the structure of XML documents. One of its characteristics is that its syntax is based on XML itself. This design decision provides a significant improvement in readability, but more important, it also allows significant reuse of technology. It is no longer necessary to write separate parsers, editors, pretty printers, and so on, to obtain a separate syntax, as was required for DTDs; any XML will do. An even more important improvement is the possibility of reusing and refining schemas. XML Schema allows one to define new types by extending or restricting already existing ones. In combination with an XML-based syntax, this feature allows one to build schemas from other schemas, thus reducing the workload. Finally, XML Schema provides a sophisticated set of data types that can be used in XML documents (DTDs were limited to strings only).

An XML schema is an element with an opening tag like

```
<xsd:schema
  xmlns:xsd="http://www.w3.org/2000/10/XMLSchema"
  version="1.0">
```

The element uses the schema of XML Schema found at the W3C Web site. It is, so to speak, the foundation on which new schemas can be built. The prefix xsd denotes the namespace of that schema (more on namespaces in the next section). If the prefix is omitted in the xmlns attribute, then we are using elements from this namespace by default:

```
<schema
  xmlns="http://www.w3.org/2000/10/XMLSchema"
  version="1.0">
```

In the following we omit the xsd prefix.

Now we turn to schema elements. Their most important contents are the definitions of element and attribute types, which are defined using data types.

**Element Types**

The syntax of element types is

```
<element name="..."/>
```

and they may have a number of optional attributes, such as types,

```
type="..." (more on types later)
```

or cardinality constraints

- minOccurs="x", where x may be any natural number (including zero)

- maxOccurs="x", where x may be any natural number (including zero) or unbounded

minOccurs and maxOccurs are generalizations of the cardinality operators ?, *, and +, offered by DTDs. When cardinality constraints are not provided explicitly, minOccurs and maxOccurs have value 1 by default.

Here are a few examples.

```
<element name="email"/>
```

```
<element name="head" minOccurs="1" maxOccurs="1"/>
```

```
<element name="to" minOccurs="1"/>
```

**Attribute Types**

The syntax of attribute types is

```
<attribute name="..."/>
```

and they may have a number of optional attributes, such as types,

```
type="..."
```

or existence (corresponds to #OPTIONAL and #IMPLIED in DTDs),

use="x", where x may be optional or required.

or a default value (corresponds to #FIXED and default values in DTDs)

use="x" value="...", where x may be default or fixed

Here are examples:

```
<attribute name="id" type="ID" use="required"/>

<element name="speaks" type="Language" use="default"
     value="en"/>
```

**Data Types**

We have already recognized the very restricted selection of data types as a key weakness of DTDs. XML Schema provides powerful capabilities for defining data type. First there is a variety of *built-in data types*. Here we list a few:

- Numerical data types, including integer, Short, Byte, Long, Float, Decimal

- String data types, including string, ID, IDREF, CDATA, Language

- Date and time data types, including time, Date, Month, Year

There are also *user-defined data types*, comprising *simple data types*, which cannot use elements or attributes, and *complex data types*, which can use elements and attributes. We discuss complex types first, deferring discussion of simple data types until we talk about restriction. Complex types are defined from already existing data types by defining some attributes (if any) and using

- sequence, a sequence of existing data type elements, the appearance of which in a predefined order is important

- all, a collection of elements that must appear, but the order of which is not important

- choice, a collection of elements, of which one will be chosen.

Here is an example:

```
<complexType name="lecturerType">
  <sequence>
    <element name="firstname" type="string"
      minOccurs="0" maxOccurs="unbounded"/>
    <element name="lastname" type="string"/>
  </sequence>
  <attribute name="title" type="string" use="optional"/>
</complexType>
```

The meaning is that an element in an XML document that is declared to be of type `lecturerType` may have a `title` attribute; it may also include any number of `firstname` elements and must include exactly one `lastname` element.

### Data Type Extension

Already existing data types can be extended by new elements or attributes. As an example, we extend the `lecturer` data type.

```
<complexType name="extendedLecturerType">
  <extension base="lecturerType">
    <sequence>
      <element name="email" type="string"
        minOccurs="0" maxOccurs="1"/>
    </sequence>
    <attribute name="rank" type="string" use="required"/>
  </extension>
</complexType>
```

In this example, `lecturerType` is extended by an `email` element and a `rank` attribute. The resulting data type looks like this:

```
<complexType name="extendedLecturerType">
  <sequence>
    <element name="firstname" type="string"
      minOccurs="0" maxOccurs="unbounded"/>
    <element name="lastname" type="string"/>
    <element name="email" type="string"
      minOccurs="0" maxOccurs="1"/>
  </sequence>
  <attribute name="title" type="string" use="optional"/>
```

```
    <attribute name="rank" type="string" use="required"/>
</complexType>
```

A hierarchical relationship exists between the original and the extended type. *Instances of the extended type are also instances of the original type.* They may contain additional information, but neither less information, nor information of the wrong type.

**Data Type Restriction**

An existing data type may also be restricted by adding constraints on certain values. For example, new `type` and `use` attributes may be added, or the numerical constraints of `minOccurs` and `maxOccurs` tightened.

It is important to understand that restriction is *not* the opposite process from extension. Restriction is not achieved by deleting elements or attributes. Therefore, the following hierarchical relationship still holds: *Instances of the restricted type are also instances of the original type.* They satisfy at least the constraints of the original type, and some new ones.

As an example, we restrict the `lecturer` data type as follows:

```
<complexType name="restrictedLecturerType">
  <restriction base="lecturerType">
    <sequence>
      <element name="firstname" type="string"
        minOccurs="1" maxOccurs="2"/>
    </sequence>
    <attribute name="title" type="string" use="required"/>
  </restriction>
</complexType>
```

The tightened constraints are shown in boldface. Readers should compare them with the original ones.

Simple data types can also be defined by restricting existing data types. For example, we can define a type `dayOfMonth` that admits values from 1 to 31 as follows:

```
<simpleType name="dayOfMonth">
  <restriction base="integer">
    <minInclusive value="1"/>
    <maxInclusive value="31"/>
  </restriction>
</simpleType>
```

It is also possible to define a data type by listing all the possible values. For example, we can define a data type dayOfWeek as follows:

```
<simpleType name="dayOfWeek">
  <restriction base="string">
    <enumeration value="Mon"/>
    <enumeration value="Tue"/>
    <enumeration value="Wed"/>
    <enumeration value="Thu"/>
    <enumeration value="Fri"/>
    <enumeration value="Sat"/>
    <enumeration value="Sun"/>
  </restriction>
</simpleType>
```

**A Concluding Example**

Here we define an XML schema for e-Mail, so that it can be compared to the DTD provided on page 36.

```
<element name="email" type="emailType"/>
<complexType name="emailType">
  <sequence>
    <element name="head" type="headType"/>
    <element name="body" type="bodyType"/>
  </sequence>
</complexType>

<complexType name="headType">
  <sequence>
    <element name="from" type="nameAddress"/>
    <element name="to" type="nameAddress"
      minOccurs="1" maxOccurs="unbounded"/>
    <element name="cc" type="nameAddress"
      minOccurs="0" maxOccurs="unbounded"/>
    <element name="subject" type="string"/>
  </sequence>
</complexType>

<complexType name="nameAddress">
  <attribute name="name" type="string" use="optional"/>
  <attribute name="address" type="string" use="required"/>
</complexType>
```

```
<complexType name="bodyType">
  <sequence>
    <element name="text" type="string"/>
    <element name="attachment" minOccurs="0"
        maxOccurs="unbounded">
      <complexType>
        <attribute name="encoding" use="default"
            value="mime">
          <simpleType>
            <restriction base="string">
              <enumeration value="mime"/>
              <enumeration value="binhex"/>
            </restriction>
          </simpleType>
        </attribute>
        <attribute name="file" type="string"
            use="required"/>
      </complexType>
    </element>
  </sequence>
</complexType>
```

Note that some data types are defined separately and given names, while others are defined within other types and defined anonymously (the types for the `attachment` element and the `encoding` attribute). In general, if a type is only used once, it makes sense to define it anonymously for local use. However, this approach reaches its limitations quickly if nesting becomes too deep.

## 2.4  Namespaces

One of the main advantages of using XML as a universal (meta) markup language is that information from various sources may be accessed; in technical terms, an XML document may use more than one DTD or schema. But since each structuring document was developed independently, *name clashes* appear inevitable. If DTD A and DTD B define an element type *e* in different ways, a parser that tries to validate an XML document in which an *e* element appears must be told which DTD to use for validation purposes.

The technical solution is simple: disambiguation is achieved by using a different prefix for each DTD or schema. The prefix is separated from the local name by a colon:

```
prefix:name
```

As an example, consider an (imaginary) joint venture of an Australian university, say, Griffith University, and an American university, say, University of Kentucky, to present a unified view for online students. Each university uses its own terminology, and there are differences. For example, lecturers in the United States are not considered regular faculty, whereas in Australia they are (in fact, they correspond to assistant professors in the United States). The following example shows how disambiguation can be achieved.

```
<?xml version="1.0" encoding="UTF-16"?>
<vu:instructors
    xmlns:vu="http://www.vu.com/empDTD"
    xmlns:gu="http://www.gu.au/empDTD"
    xmlns:uky="http://www.uky.edu/empDTD">
  <uky:faculty
    uky:title="assistant professor"
    uky:name="John Smith"
    uky:department="Computer Science"/>
  <gu:academicStaff
    gu:title="lecturer"
    gu:name="Mate Jones"
    gu:school="Information Technology"/>
</vu:instructors>
```

So, namespaces are declared within an element and can be used in that element and any of its children (elements and attributes). A namespace declaration has the form:

```
xmlns:prefix="location"
```

where location is the address of the DTD or schema. If a prefix is not specified, as in

```
xmlns="location"
```

then the location is used by default. For example, the previous example is equivalent to the following document:

```
<?xml version="1.0" encoding="UTF-16"?>
<vu:instructors
    xmlns:vu="http://www.vu.com/empDTD"
    xmlns="http://www.gu.au/empDTD"
    xmlns:uky="http://www.uky.edu/empDTD">
  <uky:faculty
    uky:title="assistant professor"
    uky:name="John Smith"
    uky:department="Computer Science"/>
  <academicStaff
    title="lecturer"
    name="Mate Jones"
    school="Information Technology"/>
</vu:instructors>
```

## 2.5 Addressing and Querying XML Documents

In relational databases, parts of a database can be selected and retrieved using query languages such as SQL. The same is true for XML documents, for which there exist a number of proposals for query languages, such as XQL, XML-QL, and XQuery.

The central concept of XML query languages is a *path expression* that specifies how a node, or a set of nodes, in the tree representation of the XML document can be reached. We introduce path expressions in the form of XPath because they can be used for purposes other than querying, namely, for transforming XML documents.

XPath is a language for addressing parts of an XML document. It operates on the tree data model of XML and has a non-XML syntax. The key concepts are path expressions. They can be

- Absolute (starting at the root of the tree); syntactically they begin with the symbol /, which refers to the root of the document, situated one level above the root element of the document;

- Relative to a context node.

Consider the following XML document:

```
<?xml version="1.0" encoding="UTF-16"?>
<!DOCTYPE library PUBLIC "library.dtd">
<library location="Bremen">
```

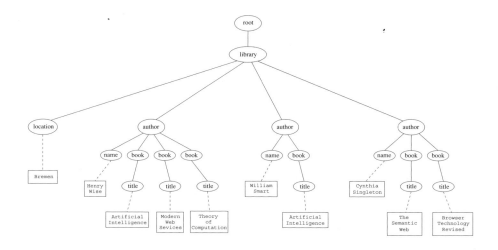

**Figure 2.2**    Tree representation of a library document

```
<author name="Henry Wise">
  <book title="Artificial Intelligence"/>
  <book title="Modern Web Services"/>
  <book title="Theory of Computation"/>
</author>
<author name="William Smart">
  <book title="Artificial Intelligence"/>
</author>
<author name="Cynthia Singleton">
  <book title="The Semantic Web"/>
  <book title="Browser Technology Revised"/>
</author>
</library>
```

Its tree representation is shown in figure 2.2.

In the following we illustrate the capabilities of XPath with a few examples of path expressions.

1. Address all `author` elements.

   ```
   /library/author
   ```

   This path expression addresses all `author` elements that are children of the `library` element node, which resides immediately below the root.

Using a sequence $/t_1/\ldots/t_n$, where each $t_{i+1}$ is a child node of $t_i$, we define a path through the tree representation.

2. An alternative solution for the previous example is

   ```
   //author
   ```

   Here `//` says that we should consider all elements in the document and check whether they are of type `author`. In other words, this path expression addresses all `author` elements anywhere in the document. Because of the specific structure of our XML document, this expression and the previous one lead to the same result; however, they may lead to different results, in general.

3. Address the `location` attribute nodes within `library` element nodes.

   ```
   /library/@location
   ```

   The symbol `@` is used to denote attribute nodes.

4. Address all `title` attribute nodes within `book` elements anywhere in the document, which have the value "`Artificial Intelligence`" (see figure 2.3).

   ```
   //book/@title="Artificial Intelligence"
   ```

5. Address all books with title "`Artificial Intelligence`" (see figure 2.4).

   ```
   //book[@title="Artificial Intelligence"]
   ```

   We call a test within square brackets a *filter expression*. It restricts the set of addressed nodes.

   Note the difference between this expression and the one in query 4. Here we address `book` elements the title of which satisfies a certain condition. In query 4 we collected `title` attribute nodes of `book` elements. A comparison of figures 2.3 and 2.4 illustrates the difference.

6. Address the first `author` element node in the XML document.

   ```
   //author[1]
   ```

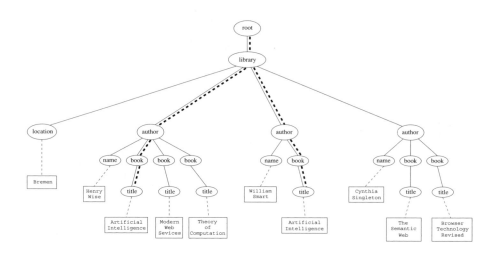

**Figure 2.3**   Tree representation of query 4

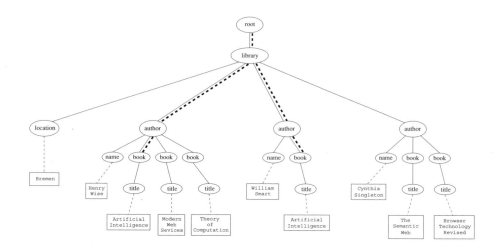

**Figure 2.4**   Tree representation of query 5

7. Address the last book element within the first author element node in the document.

```
//author[1]/book[last()]
```

8. Address all book element nodes without a title attribute.

```
//book[not @title]
```

These examples are meant to give a feeling of the expressive power of path expressions. In general, a path expression consists of a series of steps, separated by slashes. A *step* consists of an axis specifier, a node test, and an optional predicate.

- An *axis specifier* determines the tree relationship between the nodes to be addressed and the context node. Examples are parent, ancestor, child (the default), sibling, attribute node. // is such an axis specifier; it denotes descendant or self.

- A *node test* specifies which nodes to address. The most common node tests are element names (which may use namespace information), but there are others. For example, * addresses all element nodes, comment() all comment nodes, and so on.

- *Predicates* (or *filter expressions*) are optional and are used to refine the set of addressed nodes. For example, the expression [1] selects the first node, [position()=last()] selects the last node, [position() mod 2 = 0] the even nodes, and so on.

We have only presented the abbreviated syntax, XPath actually has a more complicated full syntax. References are found at the end of this chapter.

## 2.6   Processing

So far we have not provided any information about how XML documents can be displayed. Such information is necessary because unlike HTML documents, XML documents do not contain formatting information. The advantage is that a given XML document can be presented in various ways, when different *style sheets* are applied to it. For example, consider the XML element

```
<author>
  <name>Grigoris Antoniou</name>
  <affiliation>University of Bremen</affiliation>
  <email>ga@tzi.de</email>
</author>
```

The output might look like the following, if a style sheet is used:

**Grigoris Antoniou**

University of Bremen

*ga@tzi.de*

Or it might appear as follows, if a different style sheet is used:

*Grigoris Antoniou*

University of Bremen

ga@tzi.de

Style sheets can be written in various languages, for example, in CSS2 (cascading style sheets level 2). The other possibility is XSL (extensible stylesheet language).

XSL includes both a transformation language (XSLT) and a formatting language. Each of these is, of course, an XML application. XSLT specifies rules with which an input XML document is transformed to another XML document, an HTML document, or plain text. The output document may use the same DTD or schema as the input document, or it may use a completely different vocabulary.

XSLT (XSL transformations) can be used independently of the formatting language. Its ability to move data and metadata from one XML representation to another makes it a most valuable tool for XML-based applications. Generally XSLT is chosen when applications that use different DTDs or schemas need to communicate. XSLT is a tool that can be used for machine-processing of content without any regard to displaying the information for people to read. Despite this fact, in the following we use XSLT only to display XML documents.

One way of defining the presentation of an XML document is to transform it into an HTML document. Here is an example. We define an XSLT document that will be applied to the author example.

```
<?xml version="1.0" encoding="UTF-16"?>
<xsl:stylesheet version="1.0"
    xmlns:xsl="http://www.w3.org/1999/XSL/Transform">

  <xsl:template match="/author">
    <html>
      <head><title>An author< /title></head>
      <body bgcolor="white">
        <b><xsl:value-of select="name"/></b><br>
        <xsl:value-of select="affiliation"/><br>
        <i><xsl:value-of select="email"/></i>
      </body>
    </html>
  </xsl:template>
</xsl:stylesheet>
```

The output of this style sheet, applied to the previous XML document, produces the following HTML document (which now defines the presentation):

```
<html>
  <head><title>An author< /title></head>
  <body bgcolor="white">
    <b>Grigoris Antoniou</b><br>
    University of Bremen<br>
    <i>ga@tzi.de</i>
  </body>
</html>
```

Let us make a few observations. XSLT documents are XML documents. So XSLT resides on top of XML (that is, it is an XML application). The XSLT document defines a *template*; in this case an HTML document, with some placeholders for content to be inserted (see figure 2.5).

In the previous XSLT document, `xsl:value-of` retrieves the value of an element and copies it into the output document. That is, it places some content into the template.

Now suppose we had an XML document with details of several authors. It would clearly be a waste of effort to treat each `author` element separately. In such cases, a special template is defined for `author` elements, which is used by the main template. We illustrate this approach referring to the following input document:

```
<html>
<head><title>An author</title></head>
<body bgcolor="white">
  <b>...</b><br>
  ...<br>
  <i>...</i>
</body>
</html>
```

**Figure 2.5**   A template

```
<authors>
  <author>
    <name>Grigoris Antoniou</name>
    <affiliation>University of Bremen</affiliation>
    <email>ga@tzi.de</email>
  </author>
  <author>
    <name>David Billington</name>
    <affiliation>Griffith University</affiliation>
    <email>david@gu.edu.net</email>
  </author>
</authors>
```

We define the following XSLT document:

```
<?xml version="1.0" encoding="UTF-16"?>
<xsl:stylesheet version="1.0"
    xmlns:xsl="http://www.w3.org/1999/XSL/Transform">

  <xsl:template match="/">
    <html>
    <head><title>Authors< /title></head>
    <body bgcolor="white">
      <xsl:apply-templates select="authors"/>
      <!-- Apply templates for AUTHORS children -->
    </body>
    </html>
  </xsl:template>
```

```
<xsl:template match="authors">
  <xsl:apply-templates select="author"/>
</xsl:template>

<xsl:template match="author">
  <h2><xsl:value-of select="name"/></h2>
  Affiliation:<xsl:value-of select="affiliation"/><br>
  Email:  <xsl:value-of select="email"/>
  <p>
</xsl:template>
</xsl:stylesheet>
```

The output produced is

```
<html>
<head><title>Authors< /title></head>
<body bgcolor="white">
  <h2>Grigoris Antoniou</h2>
  Affiliation:  University of Bremen<br>
  Email:  ga@tzi.de
  <p>
  <h2>David Billington</h2>
  Affiliation:  Griffith University<br>
  Email:  david@gu.edu.net
  <p>
</body>
</html>
```

The `xsl:apply-templates` element causes all children of the context node to be matched against the selected path expression. For example, if the current template applies to / (that is, if the current context node is the root), then the element `xsl:apply-templates` applies to the root element, in this case, the `authors` element (remember that / is located above the root element). And if the current context node is the `authors` element, then the element `xsl:apply-templates select="author"` causes the template for the `author` elements to be applied to all `author` children of the authors element.

It is good practice to define a template for each element type in the document. Even if no specific processing is applied to certain elements, in our example `authors`, the `xsl:apply-templates` element should be used.

That way, we work our way from the root to the leaves of the tree, and all templates are indeed applied.

Now we turn our attention to attributes. Suppose we wish to process the element

```
<person firstname="John" lastname="Woo"/>
```

with XSLT. Let us attempt the easiest task imaginable, a transformation of the element to itself. One might be tempted to write

```
<xsl:template match="person">
  <person
    firstname="<xsl:value-of select="@firstname">"
    lastname="<xsl:value-of select="@lastname">"/>
</xsl:template>
```

However, this is not a well-formed XML document because tags are not allowed within the values of attributes. But the intention is clear; we wish to add attribute values into the template. In XSLT, data enclosed in curly brackets take the place of the xsl:value-of element. The correct way to define a template for this example is as follows:

```
<xsl:template match="person">
  <person
    firstname="{@firstname}"
    lastname="{@lastname}"/>
</xsl:template>
```

Finally we give a transformation example from one XML document to another, which does not specify the display. Again we use the authors document as input and define an XSLT document as follows:

```
<?xml version="1.0" encoding="UTF-16"?>
<xsl:stylesheet version="1.0"
    xmlns:xsl="http://www.w3.org/1999/XSL/Transform">

  <xsl:template match="/">
    <authors>
      <xsl:apply-templates select="authors"/>
    </authors>
  </xsl:template>
```

```
<xsl:template match="authors">
  <xsl:apply-templates select="author"/>
</xsl:template>

<xsl:template match="author">
  <author>
    <name><xsl:value-of select="name"/></name>
    <contact>
      <institute>
        <xsl:value-of select="affiliation"/>
      </institute>
      <email><xsl:value-of select="email"/></email>
    </contact>
  </author>
</xsl:template>

</xsl:stylesheet>
```

The output document should be obvious. We present its tree representation in figure 2.6 to illustrate the tree transformation character of XSLT.

## 2.7   Summary

- XML is a metalanguage that allows users to define markup for their documents using tags.

- Nesting of tags introduces structure. The structure of documents can be enforced using schemas or DTDs.

- XML separates content and structure from formatting.

- XML is the de facto standard for the representation of structured information on the Web and supports machine processing of information.

- XML supports the exchange of structured information across different applications through markup, structure, and transformations.

- XML is supported by query languages.

Some points discussed in subsequent chapters include

- The nesting of tags does not have standard meaning.

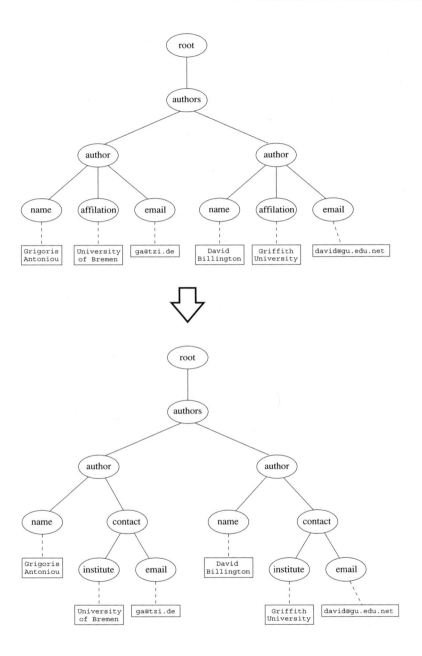

**Figure 2.6**    XSLT as tree transformation

- The semantics of XML documents is not accessible to machines, only to people.

- Collaboration and exchange are supported if there is an underlying shared understanding of the vocabulary. XML is well-suited for close collaboration, where domain- or community-based vocabularies are used. It is not so well-suited for global communication.

## Suggested Reading

Generally the official W3C documents are found at <http://www.w3.org>. Here we give a few of the most important links, together with some other useful references.

- T. Bray, J. Paoli, C. M. Sperberg-McQueen, E. Maler, eds. Extensible Markup Language (XML) 1.0, 2nd ed, W3C Recommendation, October 6, 2000. <http://www.w3.org/TR/REC-xml>.

- T. Bray, D. Hollander, A. Layman, eds. Namespaces in XML, January 14, 1999. <http://www.w3.org/TR/REC-xml-names/>.

- J. Clark, S. DeRose, eds. XML Path Language (XPath) Version 1.0, W3C Recommendation, November 16, 1999. <http://www.w3.org/TR/xpath>.

- S. Adler et al. Extensible Stylesheet Language (XSL) Version 1.0, W3C Recommendation, October 15, 2001. <http://www.w3.org/TR/xsl/>.

- J. Clark, ed. XSL Transformations (XSLT) Version 1.0, W3C Recommendation, November 16, 1999. <http://www.w3.org/TR/xslt>.

Recent trends in XML querying may be found at

- <http://www.w3.org/XML/Query.html>.

XML has attracted a lot of attention in industry, and many books covering the technicalities in depth exist. Two books for further reading on XML are

- E. R. Harold. *XML Bible*, 2nd ed. New York: Wiley (Hungry Minds), 2001.

- D. Mercer. *XML: A Beginner's Guide*. New York: McGraw Hill (Osborne), 2001.

There are several sites with teaching material on XML and related technologies:

- <http://www.xml.com>, where the following papers may be found:

  - N. Walsh. A Technical Introduction to XML. October 3, 1998.
  - T. Bray. XML Namespaces by Example. January 19, 1999.
  - E. van der Vlist. Using W3C XML Schema. October 17, 2001.
  - G. Holman. What Is XSLT? (I): The Context of XSL Transformations and the XML Path Language. August 16, 2000.

- <http://www.w3schools.com>

- <http://www.topxml.com>

- <http://www.zvon.org>

- <http://www.xslt.com>

## Exercises and Projects

2.1   In our e-mail example we specified the body of an e-mail to contain exactly one text and a number of attachments. Modify the schema to allow for an arbitrary number of texts and attachments in any order.

2.2   Search the Web for XML applications, with keywords such as "XML DTD" or "XML schema".

2.3   Read the official W3C documents on namespaces, XPath, XSL, and XSLT. Identify some issues that were not covered in this chapter, in particular, the general notation and capabilities of XPath. Write small documents that use these new aspects.

2.4   In this chapter, we did not cover links, a crucial ingredient of Web pages. XLink provides linking capabilities that go beyond HTML links. Check out XLink on the official W3C pages. Note that simple links can be created as follows:

```
<mylink xmlns:xlink=http://www.w3.org/1999/xlink"
   xlink:type="simple" xlink:href="target.html">
Click here </mylink>
```

2.5   Discuss the relevance of XSLT for defining *views* on Web sites ("views" hide certain parts of Web sites and display only those parts meant for the particular user's viewing).

2.6   Draw a comparison between document markup using XML and using TeX/LaTeX, also between XML transformations and BibTeX.

For the following projects you are asked to "design a vocabulary". This includes designing a vocabulary, writing a corresponding DTD or schema, writing sample XML documents, and transforming these documents into HTML and viewing them in a Web browser.

2.7   Design a vocabulary to model (parts of) your workplace. For example, if you are at a university, design a vocabulary about courses, teaching staff, rooms, publications, and so on.

2.8   For one of your hobbies, design a vocabulary for exchanging information with others who share your interest.

2.9   Perhaps you read books of certain categories? Design a vocabulary for describing them and communicating about them with other people.

2.10  Are you an investor? Design a vocabulary about available investment options and their properties (for example, risk, return, investor age, investor character).

2.11  Do you like cooking? Design a vocabulary about foods, tastes, and recipes.

2.12  For each of the above vocabularies, consider writing a second XSL style sheet, this time not translating the XML to HTML but instead to a different markup language, such as WML, the markup language for WAP-enabled mobile telephones. Such a style sheet should be geared toward displaying the information on small mobile devices with limited bandwidth and limited screen space. You could use one of the freely available WAP simulators to display the results.

# 3 *Describing Web Resources in RDF*

## 3.1 Introduction

XML is a universal metalanguage for defining markup. It provides a uniform framework, and a set of tools like parsers, for interchange of data and metadata between applications. However, XML does not provide any means of talking about the *semantics* (meaning) of data. For example, there is no intended meaning associated with the nesting of tags; it is up to each application to interpret the nesting. Let us illustrate this point using an example. Suppose we want to express the following fact:

> *David Billington is a lecturer of Discrete Mathematics.*

There are various ways of representing this sentence in XML. Three possibilities are

```
<course name="Discrete Mathematics">
  <lecturer>David Billington</lecturer>
</course>

<lecturer name="David Billington">
  <teaches>Discrete Mathematics</teaches>
</lecturer>

<teachingOffering>
  <lecturer>David Billington</lecturer>
  <course>Discrete Mathematics</course>
</teachingOffering>
```

Note that the first two formalizations include essentially an opposite nesting although they represent the same information. So there is no standard way of assigning meaning to tag nesting.

Although often called a "language" (and we commit this sin ourselves in this book), RDF (Resource Description Framework) is essentially a *datamodel*. Its basic building block is an object-attribute-value triple, called a *statement*. The preceding sentence about Billington is such a statement. Of course, an abstract data model needs a concrete syntax in order to be represented and transmitted, and RDF has been given a syntax in XML. As a result, it inherits the benefits associated with XML. However, it is important to understand that other syntactic representations of RDF, not based on XML, are also possible; XML-based syntax is not a necessary component of the RDF model.

RDF is domain-independent in that no assumptions about a particular domain of use are made. It is up to users to define their own terminology in a schema language called *RDF Schema* (*RDFS*). The name RDF Schema is now widely regarded as an unfortunate choice. It suggests that RDF Schema has a similar relation to RDF as XML Schema has to XML, but in fact this is not the case. XML Schema constrains the *structure* of XML documents, whereas RDF Schema defines the *vocabulary* used in RDF data models. In RDFS we can define the vocabulary, specify which properties apply to which kinds of objects and what values they can take, and describe the relationships between objects. For example, we can write

*Lecturer* is a subclass of *academic staff member*.

This sentence means that all lecturers are also academic staff members. It is important to understand that there is an intended meaning associated with "is a subclass of". It is not up to the application to interpret this term; its intended meaning must be respected by all RDF processing software. Through fixing the semantics of certain ingredients, RDF/RDFS enables us to model particular domains.

We illustrate the importance of RDF Schema with an example. Consider the following XML elements:

```
<academicStaffMember>Grigoris Antoniou</academicStaffMember>
<professor>Michael Maher</professor>
<course name="Discrete Mathematics">
  <isTaughtBy>David Billington</isTaughtBy>
</course>
```

Suppose we want to collect all academic staff members. A path expression in Xpath might be

```
//academicStaffMember
```

The result is only Grigoris Antoniou. While correct from the XML viewpoint, this answer is *semantically* unsatisfactory. Human readers would have also included Michael Maher and David Billington in the answer because

- All professors are academic staff members (that is, `professor` is a subclass of `academicStaffMember`).

- Courses are only taught by academic staff members.

This kind of information makes use of the *semantic model* of the particular domain, and cannot be represented in XML or in RDF but is typical of knowledge written in RDF Schema. Thus *RDFS makes semantic information machine-accessible*, in accordance with the Semantic Web vision.

In this chapter, sections 3.2 and 3.3 discuss RDF: the basic ideas of RDF and its XML-based syntax, and sections 3.4 and 3.5 introduce the basic concepts and the language of RDF Schema.

Section 3.6 shows the definition of some elements of the namespaces of RDF and RDF Schema. Section 3.7 presents an axiomatic semantics for RDF and RDFS. This semantics uses predicate logic and formalizes the intuitive meaning of the modeling primitives of the languages.

Section 3.8 provides a direct semantics based on inference rules, and section 3.9 is devoted to the querying of RDF/RDFS documents using RQL.

## 3.2   RDF: Basic Ideas

The fundamental concepts of RDF are resources, properties and statements.

### 3.2.1   Resources

We can think of a resource as an object, a "thing" we want to talk about. Resources may be authors, books, publishers, places, people, hotels, rooms, search queries, and so on. Every resource has a URI, a Universal Resource Identifier. A URI can be a URL (Unified Resource Locator, or Web address) or some other kind of unique identifier; note that an identifier does not necessarily enable *access* to a resource. URI schemes have been defined not only for web-locations but also for such diverse objects as telephone numbers, ISBN numbers and geographic locations. There has been a long discussion about the nature of URIs, even touching philosophical questions (for example, what is an appropriate unique identifier for a person?), but we will not go into into detail here. In general, we assume that a URI is the identifier of a Web resource.

### 3.2.2    Properties

Properties are a special kind of resources; they describe relations between resources, for example "written by", "age", "title", and so on. Properties in RDF are also identified by URIs (and in practice by URLs). This idea of using URIs to identify "things" and the relations between is quite important. This choice gives us in one stroke a global, worldwide, unique naming scheme. The use of such a scheme greatly reduces the homonym problem that has plagued distributed data representation until now.

### 3.2.3    Statements

Statements assert the properties of resources. A statement is an object-attribute-value triple, consisting of a resource, a property, and a value. Values can either be resources or *literals*. Literals are atomic values (strings), the structure of which we do not discuss further.

### 3.2.4    Three Views of a Statement

An example of a statement is

> *David Billington is the owner of the Web page*
> *http://www.cit.gu.edu.au/~db.*

The simplest way of interpreting this statement is to use the definition and consider the triple

> (http://www.cit.gu.edu.au/~db,
> http://www.mydomain.org/site-owner, #DavidBillington).

We can think of this triple $(x, P, y)$ as a logical formula $P(x, y)$, where the binary predicate $P$ relates the object $x$ to the object $y$. In fact, *RDF offers only binary predicates (properties)*. Note that the property "site-owner" and both of the two objects are identified by URLs.

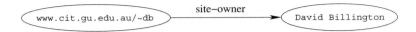

**Figure 3.1**   Graph representation of triple

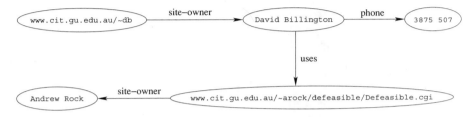

**Figure 3.2**   A semantic net

the two objects are identified by URLs, whereas the other object is simply identified by a string.

A second view is graph-based. Figure 3.1 shows the graph corresponding to the preceding statement. It is a directed graph with labeled nodes and arcs; the arcs are directed from the resource (the *subject* of the statement) to the value (the *object* of the statement). This kind of graph is known in the Artificial Intelligence community as a *semantic net* .

As we already said, the value of a statement may be a resource. Therefore, it may be linked to other resources. Consider the following triples:

( http://www.cit.gu.edu.au/∼db, http://www.mydomain.org/site-owner,
"David Billington")

( "David Billington", http://www.mydomain.org/phone, "3875507")

( "David Billington", http://www.mydomain.org/uses,
http://www.cit.gu.edu.au/∼arock/defeasible/Defeasible.cgi)

( "www.cit.gu.edu.au/∼arock/defeasible/Defeasible.cgi",
http://www.mydomain.org/site-owner, "Andrew Rock")

The graphic representation is found in figure 3.2.

Graphs are a powerful tool for human understanding. But the Semantic Web vision requires machine-accessible and machine-processable representations.

Therefore, there is a third representation possibility based on XML. According to this possibility, an RDF document is represented by an XML element with the tag `rdf:RDF`. The content of this element is a number of *descriptions*, which use `rdf:Description` tags. Every description makes a statement about a resource, which is identified in one of three different ways:

- an `about` attribute, referencing an existing resource

- an `ID` attribute, creating a new resource

- without a name, creating an anonymous resource

We will discuss the XML-based syntax of RDF in section 3.3, here we just show the representation of our first statement:

```
<?xml version="1.0" encoding="UTF-16"?>
<rdf:RDF
  xmlns:rdf="http://www.w3.org/1999/02/22-rdf-syntax-ns#"
  xmlns:mydomain="http://www.mydomain.org/my-rdf-ns">

 <rdf:Description rdf:about="http://www.cit.gu.edu.au/~db">
  <mydomain:site-owner>
   David Billington
  </mydomain:site-owner>
 </rdf:Description>

</rdf:RDF>
```

The first line specifies that we are using XML. In the following examples we omit this line, but keep in mind that it must be present in any RDF document with XML-based syntax.

The `rdf:Description` element makes a statement about the resource `http://www.cit.gu.edu.au/~db`. Within the description the property is used as a tag, and the content is the value of the property.

The descriptions are given in a certain order, in other words the XML syntax imposes a *serialization*. The order of descriptions (or resources) is *not* significant according to the abstract model of RDF. This again shows that the graph model is the real data model of RDF and that XML is just a possible serial representation of the graph.

### 3.2.5 Reification

In RDF it is possible to make statements about statements, such as

> Grigoris believes that David Billington is the creator of the Web page http://www.cit.gu.edu.au/~db.

This kind of statement can be used to describe belief or trust in in other statements, which is important in some kinds of applications. The solution is to assign a unique identifier to each statement, which can be used to refer to the statement. RDF allows this using, a *reification mechanism* (see section 3.3.6).

The key idea is to introduce an auxiliary object, say, *belief1*, and relate it to each of the three parts of the original statement through the properties *subject*, *predicate* and *object*. In the preceding example the subject of *belief1* would be *David Billington*, the predicate would be *creator*, and the object *http://www.cit.gu.edu.au/~db*. Note that this rather cumbersome approach is necessary because there are only triples in RDF; therefore we cannot add an identifier directly to a triple (then it would be a quadruple).

### 3.2.6 Data Types

Consider the telephone number "3875507". A program reading this RDF data model cannot know if the literal "3875507" is to be interpreted as an integer (an object on which it would make sense to, say, divide it by 17) or as a string, or indeed if it is a integer, whether it is in decimal or octal representation. A program can only know how to interpret this resource if the application is explicitly given the information that the literal is intended to represent a number, and which number the literal is supposed to represent. The common practice in programming languages or database systems is to provide this kind of information by associating a data type with the literal, in this case, a data type like decimal or integer. In RDF, *typed literals* are used to provide this kind of information.

Using a typed literal, we could describe David Billington's age as being the integer number 27 using the triple:

> ("David Billington", http://www.mydomain.org/age,
> "27"^^http://www.w3.org/2001/XMLSchema#integer )

This example shows two things: the use of the ^^-notation to indicate the type of a literal,[1] and the use of data types that are predefined by XML

---

1. This notation will take a different form in the XML-based syntax described in section 3.3.

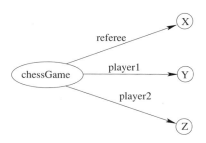

**Figure 3.3**   Representation of a tertiary predicate

Schema. Strictly speaking, the use of any externally defined data typing scheme is allowed in RDF documents, but in practice, the most widely used data typing scheme will be the one by XML Schema. XML Schema predefines a large range of data types, including Booleans, integers and floating-point numbers, times and dates.

### 3.2.7   A Critical View of RDF

We have already pointed out that RDF uses only binary properties. This restriction seems quite serious because often we use predicates with more than two arguments. Luckily, such predicates can be simulated by a number of binary predicates. We illustrate this technique for a predicate *referee* with three arguments. The intuitive meaning of *referee(X, Y, Z)* is:

> *X* is the referee in a chess game between players *Y* and *Z*.

We now introduce a new auxiliary resource *chessGame* and the binary predicates *ref*, *player1*, and *player2*. Then we can represent *referee(X, Y, Z)* as follows:

> *ref(chessGame, X)*
>
> *player1(chessGame, Y)*
>
> *player2(chessGame, Z)*

The graphic representation is shown in figure 3.3. Although the solution is sound, the problem remains that the original predicate with three arguments was simpler and more natural.

Another problem with RDF has to do with the handling of properties. As mentioned, properties are special kinds of resources. Therefore, properties themselves can be used as the object in an object-attribute-value triple (statement). While this possibility offers flexibility, it is rather unusual for modeling languages, and can be confusing for modelers.

Also, the reification mechanism is quite powerful and appears misplaced in a simple language like RDF. Making statements about statements introduces a level of complexity that is not necessary for a basic layer of the Semantic Web. Instead, it would have appeared more natural to include it in more powerful layers, which provide richer representational capabilities.

Finally, the XML-based syntax of RDF is well suited for machine processing but is not particularly human-friendly.

In summary, RDF has its idiosyncrasies and is not an optimal modeling language. However, we have to live with the fact that it is already a de facto standard. In the history of technology, often the better technology was not adopted. For example, the video system VHS was probably the technically weakest of the three systems that were available on the market at one time (the others were Beta and Video 2000), not to mention hardware and software standards in personal computing, which were arguably not adopted because of their technical merit.

On the positive side, it is true that RDF has sufficient expressive power (at least as a basis on which more layers can be built). And ultimately the Semantic Web will not be programmed in RDF, but rather with user-friendly tools that will automatically translate higher representations into RDF. Using RDF offers the benefit that information maps unambiguously to a model. And since it is likely that RDF will become a standard, the benefits of drafting data in RDF can be seen as similar to drafting information in HTML in the early days of the Web.

## 3.3   RDF: XML-Based Syntax

An RDF document consists of an `rdf:RDF` element, the content of which is a number of descriptions. For example, consider the domain of university courses and lecturers at Griffith University in the year 2001.

```
<!DOCTYPE owl [
    <!ENTITY xsd  "http://www.w3.org/2001/XMLSchema#">
]>
```

```
<rdf:RDF
  xmlns:rdf="http://www.w3.org/1999/02/22-rdf-syntax-ns#"
  xmlns:xsd="http://www.w3.org/2001/XMLSchema#"
  xmlns:uni="http://www.mydomain.org/uni-ns#">

 <rdf:Description rdf:about="949352">
  <uni:name>Grigoris Antoniou</uni:name>
  <uni:title>Professor</uni:title>
 </rdf:Description>

 <rdf:Description rdf:about="949318">
  <uni:name>David Billington</uni:name>
  <uni:title>Associate Professor</uni:title>
  <uni:age rdf:datatype="&xsd;integer">27</uni:age>
 </rdf:Description>

 <rdf:Description rdf:about="949111">
  <uni:name>Michael Maher</uni:name>
  <uni:title>Professor</uni:title>
 </rdf:Description>

 <rdf:Description rdf:about="CIT1111">
  <uni:courseName>Discrete Mathematics</uni:courseName>
  <uni:isTaughtBy>David Billington</uni:isTaughtBy>
 </rdf:Description>

 <rdf:Description rdf:about="CIT1112">
  <uni:courseName>Concrete Mathematics</uni:courseName>
  <uni:isTaughtBy>Grigoris Antoniou</uni:isTaughtBy>
 </rdf:Description>

 <rdf:Description rdf:about="CIT2112">
  <uni:courseName>Programming III</uni:courseName>
  <uni:isTaughtBy>Michael Maher</uni:isTaughtBy>
 </rdf:Description>

 <rdf:Description rdf:about="CIT3112">
  <uni:courseName>Theory of Computation</uni:courseName>
  <uni:isTaughtBy>David Billington</uni:isTaughtBy>
 </rdf:Description>

 <rdf:Description rdf:about="CIT3116">
```

```
    <uni:courseName>Knowledge Representation</uni:courseName>
    <uni:isTaughtBy>Grigoris Antoniou</uni:isTaughtBy>
  </rdf:Description>
 </rdf:RDF>
```

Let us make a few comments. First, the namespace mechanism of XML is used, but in an expanded way. In XML namespaces are only used for disambiguation purposes. In RDF external namespaces are expected to be RDF documents defining resources, which are then used in the importing RDF document. This mechanism allows the reuse of resources by other people who may decide to insert additional features into these resources. The result is the emergence of large, distributed collections of knowledge.

Second, the `rdf:about` attribute of the element `rdf:Description` is strictly speaking equivalent meaning to that of an ID attribute, but it is often used to suggest that the object about which a statement is made has already been "defined" elsewhere. Formally speaking, a set of RDF statements together simply forms a large graph, relating things to other things through properties, and there is no such thing as "defining" an object in one place and referring to it elsewhere. Nevertheless, in the serialized XML syntax, it is sometimes useful (if only for human readability) to suggest that one location in the XML serialization is the "defining" location, while other locations state "additional" properties about an object that has been "defined" elsewhere.

In fact the preceding example is slightly misleading. If we wanted to be absolutely correct, we should replace all occurrences of course and staff ID's, such as 949352 and CIT3112, by references to the external namespace, for example

```
  <rdf:Description
    rdf:about="http://www.mydomain.org/uni-ns/#CIT3112">
```

We have refrained from doing so to improve readability of our initial example because we are primarily interested here in the ideas of RDF. However, readers should be aware that this would be the precise way of writing a correct RDF document.

The content of `rdf:Description` elements are called *property elements*. For example, in the description

```
  <rdf:Description rdf:about="CIT3116">
   <uni:courseName>Knowledge Representation</uni:courseName>
   <uni:isTaughtBy>Grigoris Antoniou</uni:isTaughtBy>
  </rdf:Description>
```

the two elements uni:courseName and uni:isTaughtBy both define property-value pairs for CIT3116. The preceding description corresponds to two RDF statements.

Third, the attribute rdf:datatype="&xsd;integer" is used to indicate the data type of the value of the age property. Even though the age property has been defined to have "&xsd;integer" as its range, it is still required to indicate the type of the value of this property each time it is used. This is to ensure that an RDF processor can assign the correct type of the property value even if it has not seen the corresponding RDF Schema definition before (a scenario that is quite likely to occur in the unrestricted World Wide Web).

Finally, the property elements of a description must be read conjunctively. In the preceding example, the subject is called "Knowledge Representation" *and* is taught by Grigoris Antoniou.

### 3.3.1   The rdf:resource Attribute

The preceding example was not satisfactory in one respect: the relationships between courses and lecturers were not formally defined but existed implicitly through the use of the same name. To a machine, the use of the same name may just be a coincidence: for example, the David Billington who teaches CIT3112 may not be the same person as the person with ID 949318 who happens to be called David Billington. What we need instead is a formal specification of the fact that, for example, the teacher of CIT1111 is the staff member with number 949318, whose name is David Billington. We can achieve this effect using an rdf:resource attribute:

```
<rdf:Description rdf:about="CIT1111">
 <uni:courseName>Discrete Mathematics</uni:courseName>
 <uni:isTaughtBy rdf:resource="949318"/>
</rdf:Description>

<rdf:Description rdf:about="949318">
 <uni:name>David Billington</uni:name>
 <uni:title>Associate Professor</uni:title>
</rdf:Description>
```

We note that in case we had *defined* the resource of the staff member with ID number 939318 in the RDF document using the ID attribute instead of the about attribute, we would have had to use a # symbol in front of 949318 in the value of rdf:resource:

```
<rdf:Description rdf:about="CIT1111">
  <uni:courseName>Discrete Mathematics</uni:courseName>
  <uni:isTaughtBy rdf:resource="#949318"/>
</rdf:Description>

<rdf:Description rdf:ID="#949318">
  <uni:name>David Billington</uni:name>
  <uni:title>Associate Professor</uni:title>
</rdf:Description>
```

The same is true for externally defined resources: For example, we refer to the externally defined resource CIT1111 by using

```
http://www.mydomain.org/uni-ns/#CIT1111
```

as the value of rdf:about, where www.mydomain.org/uni-ns/ is the URI where the definition of CIT1111 is found. In other words, a description with an ID defines a fragment URI, which can be used to reference the defined description.

### 3.3.2  Nested Descriptions

Descriptions may be defined within other descriptions. For example, we may replace the descriptions of the previous example with the following, nested description:

```
<rdf:Description rdf:about="CIT1111">
 <uni:courseName>Discrete Mathematics</uni:courseName>
 <uni:isTaughtBy>
  <rdf:Description rdf:about="949318">
   <uni:name>David Billington</uni:name>
   <uni:title>Associate Professor</uni:title>
  </rdf:Description>
 </uni:isTaughtBy>
</rdf:Description>
```

Other courses, such as CIT3112, can still refer to the new resource 949318. In other words, although a description may be defined within another description, its scope is global.

### 3.3.3  The rdf:type Element

In our examples so far, the descriptions fall into two categories: courses and lecturers. This fact is clear to human readers, but has not been formally declared anywhere, so it is not accessible to machines. In RDF it is possible to make such statements using the `rdf:type` element. Here are a couple of descriptions that include typing information.

```
<rdf:Description rdf:about="CIT1111">
<rdf:type rdf:resource="&uni;course"/>
  <uni:courseName>Discrete Mathematics</uni:courseName>
  <uni:isTaughtBy rdf:resource="949318"/>
</rdf:Description>

<rdf:Description rdf:about="949318">
 <rdf:type rdf:resource="&uni;lecturer"/>
 <uni:name>David Billington</uni:name>
 <uni:title>Associate Professor</uni:title>
</rdf:Description>
```

Note that `rdf:type` allows us to introduce some structure to the RDF document. More structuring possibilities are introduced later in this chapter when we discuss RDF Schema.

### 3.3.4    Abbreviated Syntax

It is possible to abbreviate the syntax of RDF documents. The simplification rules are

1. Childless property elements within description elements may be replaced by XML attributes, as in XML.

2. For description elements with a typing element we can use the name specified in the `rdf:type` element instead of `rdf:Description`.

For example, the description

```
<rdf:Description rdf:ID="CIT1111">
 <rdf:type rdf:resource="&uni;course"/>
 <uni:courseName>Discrete Mathematics</uni:courseName>
 <uni:isTaughtBy rdf:resource="#949318"/>
</rdf:Description>
```

is (according to rule 1 applied to `uni:courseName`) equivalent to

```
<rdf:Description rdf:ID="CIT1111"
  uni:courseName="Discrete Mathematics">
```

```
  <rdf:type rdf:resource="&uni;course"/>
  <uni:isTaughtBy rdf:resource="#949318"/>
</rdf:Description>
```

and also (by rule 2) to

```
<uni:course rdf:ID="CIT1111"
            uni:courseName="Discrete Mathematics">
 <uni:isTaughtBy rdf:resource="#949318"/>
</uni:course>
```

Keep in mind that these three representations are just syntactic variations of
the same RDF statement. That is, they are equivalent according to the RDF
data model, although they have different XML syntax.

### 3.3.5  Container Elements

Container elements are used to collect a number of resources or attributes
about which we want to make statements *as a whole*. In our example, we may
wish to talk about the courses given by a particular lecturer. Three types of
containers are available in RDF:

rdf:Bag  an unordered container, which may contain multiple occurrences
(not true for a set). Typical examples are members of the faculty board
and documents in a folder — examples where an order is not imposed.

rdf:Seq  an ordered container, which may contain multiple occurrences.
Typical examples are the modules of a course, items on an agenda, an
alphabetized list of staff members — examples where an order is imposed.

rdf:Alt  a set of alternatives. Typical examples are the document home
and mirrors, and translations of a document in various languages.

The content of container elements are elements which are named rdf:_1,
rdf:_2, and so on. Let us reformulate our entire RDF document.

```
<rdf:RDF
  xmlns:rdf="http://www.w3.org/1999/02/22-rdf-syntax-ns#"
  xmlns:uni="http://www.mydomain.org/uni-ns#">

 <uni:lecturer rdf:about="949352"
               uni:name="Grigoris Antoniou"
               uni:title="Professor">
```

```
  <uni:coursesTaught>
   <rdf:Bag>
    <rdf:_1 rdf:resource="CIT1112"/>
    <rdf:_2 rdf:resource="CIT3116"/>
   </rdf:Bag>
  </uni:coursesTaught>
 </uni:lecturer>

 <uni:lecturer rdf:about="949318"
               uni:name="David Billington"
               uni:title="Associate Professor">
  <uni:coursesTaught>
   <rdf:Bag>
    <rdf:_1 rdf:resource="CIT1111"/>
    <rdf:_2 rdf:resource="CIT3112"/>
   </rdf:Bag>
  </uni:coursesTaught>
 </uni:lecturer>

 <uni:lecturer rdf:about="949111"
               uni:name="Michael Maher"
               uni:title="Professor">
  <uni:coursesTaught rdf:resource="CIT2112"/>
 </uni:lecturer>

 <uni:course rdf:about="CIT1111"
             uni:courseName="Discrete Mathematics">
  <uni:isTaughtBy rdf:resource="949318"/>
 </uni:course>

 <uni:course rdf:about="CIT1112"
             uni:courseName="Concrete Mathematics">
  <uni:isTaughtBy rdf:resource="949352"/>
 </uni:course>

 <uni:course rdf:about="CIT2112"
             uni:courseName="Programming III">
  <uni:isTaughtBy rdf:resource="949111"/>
 </uni:course>

 <uni:course rdf:about="CIT3112"
             uni:courseName="Theory of Computation">
```

```
  <uni:isTaughtBy rdf:resource="949318"/>
</uni:course>

<uni:course rdf:about="CIT3116"
            uni:courseName="Knowledge Representation">
  <uni:isTaughtBy rdf:resource="949352"/>
</uni:course>


</rdf:RDF>
```

Instead of `rdf:_1`, `rdf:_2` ...it is possible to write `rdf:li`. We use this syntactic variant in the following example. Suppose the course CIT1111 is taught by either Grigoris Antoniou or David Billington:

```
<uni:course rdf:about="CIT1111"
            uni:courseName="Discrete Mathematics">
  <uni:lecturer>
   <rdf:Alt>
    <rdf:li rdf:resource="949352"/>
    <rdf:li rdf:resource="949318"/>
   </rdf:Alt>
  </uni:lecturer>
</uni:course>
```

The container elements have an optional `ID` attribute, with which the container can be identified and referred to:

```
<uni:lecturer rdf:about="949318"
              uni:name="David Billington"
              uni:title="Associate Professor">
  <uni:coursesTaught>
   <rdf:Bag rdf:ID="DBcourses">
    <rdf:_1 rdf:resource="CIT1111"/>
    <rdf:_2 rdf:resource="CIT3112"/>
   </rdf:Bag>
  </uni:coursesTaught>
</uni:lecturer>
```

A typical application of container elements is the representation of predicates with more than two arguments. We reconsider the example *referee(X, Y, Z)*, where $X$ is the referee of a chess game between players $Y$ and $Z$. One solution is to distinguish the referee $X$ from the players $Y$ and $Z$. The graphic representation is found in figure 3.4. The solution in XML-based syntax looks like this:

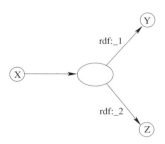

**Figure 3.4**   Representation of a tertiary predicate

```
<referee rdf:about=". . .#X">
 <players>
  <rdf:Bag>
   <rdf:li rdf:resource=". . .#Y"/>
   <rdf:li rdf:resource=". . .#Z"/>
  </rdf:Bag>
 </players>
</referee>
```

Note that `rdf:Bag` defines an anonymous auxiliary resource. We chose to use a bag because we assumed that no distinction between the players is made. If order were important, say the first-named player has White and the second Black, we would use a sequence instead.

A limitation of these containers is that there is no way to close them, to say "these are all the members of the container". This is because, while one graph may describe some of the members, there is no way to exclude the possibility that there is another graph somewhere that describes additional members. RDF provides support for describing groups containing only the specified members, in the form of RDF collections. An RDF collection is a group of things represented as a list structure in the RDF graph. This list structure is constructed using a predefined collection vocabulary consisting of the predefined type `rdf:List`, the predefined properties `rdf:first` and `rdf:rest`, and the predefined resource `rdf:nil`. This allows us to write

```
<rdf:Description rdf:about="CIT2112">
 <uni:isTaughtBy>
  <rdf:List>
   <rdf:first>
    <rdf:Description rdf:about="949111"/>
   </rdf:first>
   <rdf:rest>
    <rdf:List>
     <rdf:first>
      <rdf:Description rdf:about="949352"/>
     </rdf:first>
     <rdf:rest>
      <rdf:List>
       <rdf:first>
        <rdf:Description rdf:about="949318"/>
       </rdf:first>
       <rdf:rest>
        <rdf:Description rdf:about="&rdf;nil"/>
       </rdf:rest>
      </rdf:List>
     </rdf:rest>
    </rdf:List>
   </rdf:rest>
  </rdf:List>
 </uni:isTaughtBy>
</rdf:Description>
```

This states that `CIT2112` is taught by teachers identified as the resources `949111`, `949352`, and `949318`, *and nobody else* (indicated by the terminator symbol `nil`). A shorthand syntax for this has been defined, using the "`Collection`" value for the `rdf:parseType` attribute:

```
<rdf:Description rdf:about="CIT2112">
  <uni:isTaughtBy rdf:parseType="Collection">
    <rdf:Description rdf:about="949111"/>
    <rdf:Description rdf:about="949352"/>
    <rdf:Description rdf:about="949318"/>
  </uni:isTaughtBy>
</rdf:Description>
```

### 3.3.6    Reification

As we have said, sometimes we wish to make statements about other statements. To do so we must be able to refer to a statement using an identifier. RDF allows such reference through a reification mechanism which turns a statement into a resource. For example, the description

```
<rdf:Description rdf:about="949352">
 <uni:name>Grigoris Antoniou</uni:name>
</rdf:Description>
```

reifies as

```
<rdf:Statement rdf:about="StatementAbout949352">
 <rdf:subject rdf:resource="949352"/>
 <rdf:predicate rdf:resource="&uni;name"/>
 <rdf:object>Grigoris Antoniou</rdf:object>
</rdf:Statement>
```

Note that `rdf:subject`, `rdf:predicate`, and `rdf:object` allow us to access the parts of a statement.

The ID of the statement can be used to refer to it, as can be done for any description. We can either write an `rdf:Description` if we don't want to talk about it further, or an `rdf:Statement` if we wish to refer to it.

If more than one property element is contained in a description element, the elements correspond to more than one statement. These statements can either be placed in a bag and referred to as an entity, or they can reify separately (see exercise 3.1).

## 3.4    RDF Schema: Basic Ideas

RDF is a universal language that lets users describe resources using their own vocabularies. RDF does not make assumptions about any particular application domain, nor does it define the semantics of any domain. Is it up to the user to do so in RDF Schema (RDFS).

### 3.4.1    Classes and Properties

How do we describe a particular domain? Let us consider the domain of courses and lecturers at Griffith University. First we have to specify the "things" we want to talk about. Here we make a first, fundamental distinction. On one hand, we want to talk about particular lecturers, such as David

Billington, and particular courses, such as Discrete Mathematics; we have already done so in RDF. But we also want to talk about courses, first-year courses, lecturers, professors, and so on. What is the difference? In the first case we talk about *individual objects* (resources), in the second we talk about *classes* that define types of objects.

A class can be thought of as a set of elements. Individual objects that belong to a class are referred to as *instances* of that class. We have already defined the relationship between instances and classes in RDF using `rdf:type`.

An important use of classes is to impose restrictions on what can be stated in an RDF document using the schema. In programming languages, *typing* is used to prevent nonsense from being written (such as $A + 1$, where $A$ is an array; we lay down that the arguments of $+$ must be numbers). The same is needed in RDF. After all, we would like to disallow statements such as

Discrete Mathematics is taught by Concrete Mathematics.
Room MZH5760 is taught by David Billington.

The first statement is nonsensical because we want courses to be taught by lecturers only. This imposes a restriction on the values of the property "is taught by". In mathematical terms, we restrict the *range* of the property.

The second statement is nonsensical because only courses can be taught. This imposes a restriction on the objects to which the property can be applied. In mathematical terms, we restrict the *domain* of the property.

### 3.4.2   Class Hierarchies and Inheritance

Once we have classes we would also like to establish relationships between them. For example, suppose that we have classes for

| | |
|---|---|
| staff members | assistant professors |
| academic staff members | administrative staff members |
| professors | technical support staff members |
| associate professors | |

These classes are not unrelated to each other. For example, every professor is an academic staff member. We say that "professor" is a *subclass* of "academic staff member", or equivalently, that "academic staff member" is a *superclass* of "professor". The subclass relationship defines a hierarchy of classes, as shown in figure 3.5. In general, $A$ is a subclass of $B$ if every instance of $A$ is also an instance of $B$. There is no requirement in RDF Schema that the classes

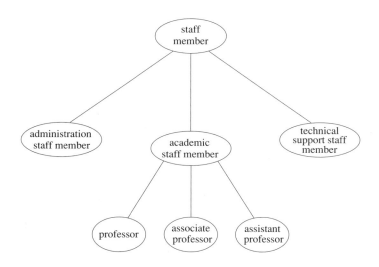

**Figure 3.5**   A hierarchy of classes

together form a strict hierarchy. In other words, a subclass graph as in figure 3.5 need not be a tree. A class may have multiple superclasses. If a class $A$ is a subclass of both $B_1$ and $B_2$, this simply means that every instance of $A$ is both an instance of $B_1$ and an instance of $B_2$.

A hierarchical organization of classes has a very important practical significance, which we outline now. Consider the range restriction

Courses must be taught by academic staff members only.

Suppose Michael Maher were defined as a professor. Then, according to the preceding restriction, he is not allowed to teach courses. The reason is that there is no statement specifying that Michael Maher is also an academic staff member. It would be counterintuitive to overcome this difficulty by adding that statement to our description. Instead we would like Michael Maher to *inherit* the ability to teach from the class of academic staff members. Exactly this is done in RDF Schema.

By doing so, RDF Schema *fixes the semantics* of "is a subclass of". Now it is not up to an application to interpret "is a subclass of"; instead its intended meaning must be used by all RDF processing software. By making such semantic definitions RDFS is a (still limited), language for defining the semantics of particular domains. Stated another way, RDF Schema is a primitive *ontology* language.

Classes, inheritance, and properties are, of course, known in other fields of computing, for example in object-oriented programming. But while there are many similarities, there are differences, too. In object-oriented programming, an object class defines the properties that apply to it. To add new properties to a class means to modify the class.

However, in RDFS, properties are defined globally, that is, they are not encapsulated as attributes in class definitions. It is possible to define new properties that apply to an existing class without changing that class.

On one hand, this is a powerful mechanism with far-reaching consequences: we may use classes defined by others and adapt them to our requirements through new properties. On the other hand, this handling of properties deviates from the standard approach that has emerged in the area of modeling and object-oriented programming. It is another idiosyncratic feature of RDF/RDFS.

### 3.4.3 Property Hierarchies

We saw that hierarchical relationships between classes can be defined. The same can be done for properties. For example, "is taught by" is a *subproperty* of "involves". If a course $c$ is taught by an academic staff member $a$, then $c$ also involves $a$. The converse is not necessarily true. For example, $a$ may be the convener of the course, or a tutor who marks student homework but does not teach $c$.

In general, $P$ is a subproperty of $Q$ if $Q(x, y)$ whenever $P(x, y)$.

### 3.4.4 RDF versus RDFS Layers

As a final point, we illustrate the different layers involved in RDF and RDFS using a simple example. Consider the RDF statement

Discrete Mathematics is taught by David Billington.

The schema for this statement may contain classes such as lecturers, academic staff members, staff members, first-year courses, and properties such as is taught by, involves, phone, employee id. Figure 3.6 illustrates the layers of RDF and RDF Schema for this example. In this figure, blocks are properties, ellipses above the dashed line are classes, and ellipses below the dashed line are instances.

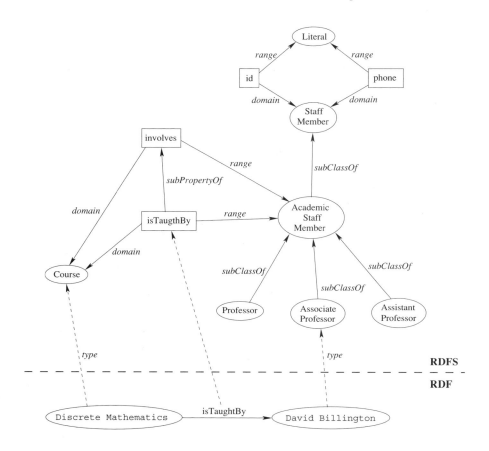

**Figure 3.6**   RDF and RDFS layers

The schema in figure 3.6 is itself written in a formal language, RDF Schema, that can express its ingredients: `subClassOf`, `Class`, `Property`, `subPropertyOf`, `Resource`, and so on. Next we describe the language of RDF Schema in more detail.

## 3.5   RDF Schema: The Language

RDF Schema provides modeling primitives for expressing the information described in section 3.4. One decision that must be made is what formal language to use. It should not be surprising that RDF itself will be used: the modeling primitives of RDF Schema are defined using resources and properties. This choice can be justified by looking at figure 3.6: we presented this figure as displaying a class/property hierarchy plus instances, but it is, of course, itself simply a labeled graph that can be encoded in RDF. Remember that RDF allows one to express any statement about any resource, and that anything that has a URI can be a resource. So, if we wish to say that the class "lecturer" is a subclass of "academic staff member", we may

1. define resources `lecturer`, `academicStaffMember`, and `subClassOf`

2. define `subClassOf` to be a property

3. write the triple (`subClassOf`, `lecturer`, `academicStaffMember`)

All these steps are within the capabilities of RDF. So, an RDFS document (that is an RDF schema) is just an RDF document, and we use the XML-based syntax of RDF. In particular, all syntactic definitions of section 3.3 must be followed.

Now we define the modeling primitives of RDF Schema.

### 3.5.1   Core Classes

The core classes are

`rdfs:Resource`, the class of all resources.

`rdfs:Class`, the class of all classes.

`rdfs:Literal`, the class of all literals (strings). At present, literals form the only "data type" of RDF/RDFS.

`rdf:Property`, the class of all properties.

`rdf:Statement`, the class of all reified statements.

For example, a class `lecturer` can be defined as follows:

```
<rdfs:Class rdf:ID="lecturer">
  ...
</rdfs:Class>
```

### 3.5.2    Core Properties for Defining Relationships

The core properties for defining relationships are

rdf:type, which relates a resource to its class (see section 3.3.3). The resource is declared to be an instance of that class.

rdfs:subClassOf, which relates a class to one of its superclasses; all instances of a class are instances of its superclass. Note that a class may be
a subclass of more than one class. As an example, the class femalePro-
fessor may be a subclass of both female and professor.

rdfs:subPropertyOf, which relates a property to one of its superprop-
erties.

Here is an example stating that all lecturers are staff members:

```
<rdfs:Class rdf:about="lecturer">
 <rdfs:subClassOf rdf:resource="staffMember"/>
</rdfs:Class>
```

Note that rdfs:subClassOf and rdfs:subPropertyOf are transitive,
by definition. Also, it is interesting that rdfs:Class is a subclass of
rdfs:Resource (every class is a resource), and rdfs:Resource is an instance of rdfs:Class (rdfs:Resource is the class of all resources, so it is
a class!). For the same reason, every class is an instance of rdfs:Class.

### 3.5.3    Core Properties for Restricting Properties

The core properties for restricting properties are

rdfs:domain, which specifies the domain of a property $P$, that is, the class
of those resources that may appear as subjects in a triple with predicate
$P$. If the domain is not specified, then any resource can be the subject.

rdfs:range, which specifies the range of a property $P$, that is, the class of
those resources that may appear as values in a triple with predicate $P$.

Here is an example, stating that phone applies to staff members only and
that its value is always a literal.

```
<rdf:Property rdf:ID="phone">
 <rdfs:domain rdf:resource="#staffMember"/>
 <rdfs:range rdf:resource="&rdf;Literal"/>
</rdf:Property>
```

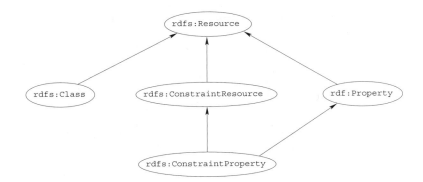

**Figure 3.7** Subclass hierarchy of some modeling primitives of RDFS

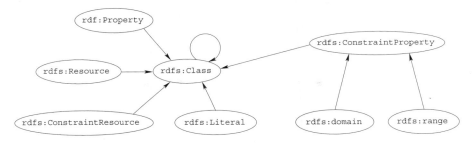

**Figure 3.8** Instance relationships of some modeling primitives of RDFS

In RDF Schema there are also

rdfs:ConstraintResource, the class of all constraints

rdfs:ConstraintProperty, which contains all properties that define constraints. It has only two instances, rdfs:domain and rdfs:range. It is defined to be a subclass of rdfs:ConstraintResource and rdf:Property

Figures 3.7 and 3.8 show the relationships between core modeling primitives in RDFS.

### 3.5.4    Useful Properties for Reification

The following are some useful properties for reification (see section 3.3.6):

`rdf:subject,`  which relates a reified statement to its subject

`rdf:predicate,`  which relates a reified statement to its predicate

`rdf:object,`  which relates a reified statement to its object

### 3.5.5    Container Classes

As mentioned in section 3.3.5, the container elements are

`rdf:Bag,`  the class of bags

`rdf:Seq,`  the class of sequences

`rdf:Alt,`  the class of alternatives.

`rdfs:Container,`  which is a superclass of all container classes, including
the three preceding ones.

### 3.5.6    Utility Properties

A resource may be defined and described in many places on the Web. The
following properties allow us to define links to those addresses:

`rdfs:seeAlso`  relates a resource to another resource that explains it

`rdfs:isDefinedBy`  is a subproperty of `rdfs:seeAlso` and relates a resource to the place where its definition, typically an RDF schema, is found.

Often it is useful to provide more information, intended for human readers.
This can be done with the following properties:

`rdfs:comment.`  Comments, typically longer text, can be associated with a
resource.

`rdfs:label.`  A human-friendly label (name) is associated with a resource.
Among other purposes, it may serve as the name of a node in a graphic
representation of the RDF document.

### 3.5.7 Example: A University

We refer to the courses and lecturers example, and provide a conceptual model of the domain, that is, an ontology.

```
<rdf:RDF
  xmlns:rdf="http://www.w3.org/1999/02/22-rdf-syntax-ns#"
  xmlns:rdfs="http://www.w3.org/2000/01/rdf-schema#">

<rdfs:Class rdf:ID="lecturer">
 <rdfs:comment>
  The class of lecturers
  All lecturers are academic staff members.
 </rdfs:comment>
 <rdfs:subClassOf rdf:resource="#academicStaffMember"/>
</rdfs:Class>

<rdfs:Class rdf:ID="academicStaffMember">
 <rdfs:comment>
  The class of academic staff members
 </rdfs:comment>
 <rdfs:subClassOf rdf:resource="#staffMember"/>
</rdfs:Class>

<rdfs:Class rdf:ID="staffMember">
 <rdfs:comment>The class of staff members</rdfs:comment>
</rdfs:Class>

<rdfs:Class rdf:ID="course">
 <rdfs:comment>The class of courses</rdfs:comment>
</rdfs:Class>

<rdf:Property rdf:ID="involves">
 <rdfs:comment>
  It relates only courses to lecturers.
 </rdfs:comment>
 <rdfs:domain rdf:resource="#course"/>
 <rdfs:range rdf:resource="#lecturer"/>
</rdf:Property>

<rdf:Property rdf:ID="isTaughtBy">
 <rdfs:comment>
  Inherits its domain ("course") and range ("lecturer")
```

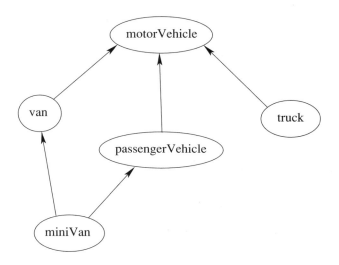

**Figure 3.9**  Class hierarchy for the motor vehicles example

```
   from its superproperty "involves"
 </rdfs:comment>
 <rdfs:subPropertyOf rdf:resource="#involves"/>
 </rdf:Property>

<rdf:Property rdf:ID="phone">
 <rdfs:comment>
  It is a property of staff members
  and takes literals as values.
 </rdfs:comment>
 <rdfs:domain rdf:resource="#staffMember"/>
 <rdfs:range rdf:resource="&rdf;Literal"/>
 </rdf:Property>
</rdf:RDF>
```

### 3.5.8   Example: Motor Vehicles

Here we present a simple ontology of motor vehicles. The class relationships are shown in figure 3.9.

```
<rdf:RDF
  xmlns:rdf="http://www.w3.org/1999/02/22-rdf-syntax-ns#"
```

```
 xmlns:rdfs="http://www.w3.org/2000/01/rdf-schema#">

<rdfs:Class rdf:ID="motorVehicle"/>

<rdfs:Class rdf:ID="van">
 <rdfs:subClassOf rdf:resource="#motorVehicle"/>
</rdfs:Class>

<rdfs:Class rdf:ID="truck">
 <rdfs:subClassOf rdf:resource="#motorVehicle"/>
</rdfs:Class>

<rdfs:Class rdf:ID="passengerVehicle">
 <rdfs:subClassOf rdf:resource="#motorVehicle"/>
</rdfs:Class>

<rdfs:Class rdf:ID="miniVan">
 <rdfs:subClassOf rdf:resource="#passengerVehicle"/>
 <rdfs:subClassOf rdf:resource="#van"/>
</rdfs:Class>
</rdf:RDF>
```

## 3.6 RDF and RDF Schema in RDF Schema

Now that we know the main components of the RDF and RDFS languages, it may be instructive to look at the definitions of RDF and RDFS. These definitions are expressed in the language of RDF Schema. One task is to see how easily they can be read now that the meaning of each component has been clarified.

The following definitions are just part of the full language specification. The remaining parts are found in the namespaces specified in `rdf:RDF`.

### 3.6.1 RDF

```
<?xml version="1.0" encoding="UTF-16"?>
<rdf:RDF
  xmlns:rdf="http://www.w3.org/1999/02/22-rdf-syntax-ns#"
  xmlns:rdfs="http://www.w3.org/2000/01/rdf-schema#">

 <rdfs:Class rdf:ID="Statement"
  rdfs:comment="The class of triples consisting of a
```

```
                                  predicate, a subject and an object
                                  (that is, a reified statement)"/>

            <rdfs:Class rdf:ID="Property"
             rdfs:comment="The class of properties"/>

            <rdfs:Class rdf:ID="Bag"
             rdfs:comment="The class of unordered collections"/>

            <rdfs:Class rdf:ID="Seq"
             rdfs:comment="The class of ordered collections"/>

            <rdfs:Class rdf:ID="Alt"
             rdfs:comment="The class of collections of alternatives"/>

            <rdf:Property rdf:ID="predicate"
             rdfs:comment="Identifies the property used in a statement
                           when representing the statement
        in reified form">
             <rdfs:domain rdf:resource="#Statement"/>
             <rdfs:range rdf:resource="#Property"/>
            </rdf:Property>

            <rdf:Property rdf:ID="subject"
             rdfs:comment="Identifies the resource that a statement is
                           describing when representing the statement
                           in reified form">
             <rdfs:domain rdf:resource="#Statement"/>
            </rdf:Property>

            <rdf:Property rdf:ID="object"
             rdfs:comment="Identifies the object of a statement
                           when representing the statement
                           in reified form"/>

            <rdf:Property rdf:ID="type"
             rdfs:comment="Identifies the class of a resource.
                           The resource is an instance
        of that class."/>

            </rdf:RDF>
```

## 3.6.2  RDF Schema

```
<rdf:RDF
  xmlns:rdf="http://www.w3.org/1999/02/22-rdf-syntax-ns#"
  xmlns:rdfs="http://www.w3.org/2000/01/rdf-schema#">

<rdfs:Class rdf:ID="Resource"
  rdfs:comment="The most general class"/>

<rdfs:Class rdf:ID="comment"
  rdfs:comment="Use this for descriptions">
  <rdfs:domain rdf:resource="#Resource"/>
  <rdfs:range rdf:resource="#Literal"/>
</rdfs:Class>

<rdfs:Class rdf:ID="Class"
  rdfs:comment="The concept of classes.
                All classes are resources">
  <rdfs:subClassOf rdf:resource="#Resource"/>
</rdfs:Class>

<rdf:Property rdf:ID="subClassOf">
  <rdfs:domain rdf:resource="#Class"/>
  <rdfs:range rdf:resource="#Class"/>
</rdf:Property>

<rdf:Property rdf:ID="subPropertyOf">
  <rdfs:domain rdf:resource="&rdf;Property"/>
  <rdfs:range rdf:resource="&rdf;Property"/>
</rdf:Property>

</rdf:RDF>
```

The namespaces do *not* provide the full definition of RDF and RDF Schema. Consider, for example, `rdfs:subClassOf`. The namespace specifies only that it applies to classes and has a class as a value. The meaning of being a subclass, namely, that all instances of one class are also instances of its superclass, is not expressed anywhere. In fact, it cannot be expressed in an RDF document. If it could, there would be no need for defining RDF Schema.

We provide a formal semantics in the next section. Of course, RDF parsers and other software tools for RDF (including query processors) must be aware of the full semantics.

## 3.7    An Axiomatic Semantics for RDF and RDF Schema

In this section we formalize the meaning of the modeling primitives of RDF and RDF Schema. Thus we capture the *semantics* of RDF and RDFS.

The formal language we use is *predicate logic,* universally accepted as the foundation of all (symbolic) knowledge representation. Formulas used in the formalization are referred to as *axioms*.

By describing the semantics of RDF and RDFS in a formal language like logic we make the semantics unambiguous and machine accessible. Also, we provide a basis for reasoning support by automated reasoners manipulating logical formulas.

### 3.7.1    The Approach

All language primitives in RDF and RDF Schema are represented by constants: $Resource, Class, Property, subClassOf$, and so on. A few predefined predicates are used as a foundation for expressing relationships between the constants.

An auxiliary theory of lists is used. It has function symbols

$nil$   (empty list)

$cons(x, l)$   (adds an element to the front of the list)

$first(l)$   (returns the first element)

$rest(l)$   (returns the rest of the list)

and predicate symbols

$item(x, l)$   (tests if an element occurs in the list)

$list(l)$   (tests whether $l$ is a list)

Lists are used to represent containers in RDF. They are also needed to capture the meaning of certain constructs (such as cardinality constraints) in richer ontology languages.

Most axioms provide typing information. For example,

$Type(subClassOf, Property)$

says that $subClassOf$ is a property. We use predicate logic with equality. Variable names begin with ?. All axioms are implicitly universally quantified.

Here we show the definition of most elements of RDF and RDF Schema. The axiomatic semantics of the full languages is found in an online document; see reference (Fikes and McGuinness 2001).

### 3.7.2   Basic Predicates

The basic precicates are

$PropVal(P, R, V)$, a predicate with three arguments, which is used to represent an RDF statement with resource $R$, property $P$ and value $V$

$Type(R, T)$, short for $PropVal(type, R, T)$, which specifies that the resource $R$ has the type $T$

$$Type(?r, ?t) \longleftrightarrow PropVal(type, ?r, ?t)$$

### 3.7.3   RDF

An RDF statement (triple) $(P, R, V)$ is represented as $PropVal(P, R, V)$.

#### Classes

In our language we have constants $Class, Resource, Property, Literal$. All classes are instances of $Class$, that is, they have the type $Class$:

$$Type(Class, Class)$$
$$Type(Resource, Class)$$
$$Type(Property, Class)$$
$$Type(Literal, Class)$$

$Resource$ is the most general class: every object is a resource. Therefore, every class and every property is a resource:

$$Type(?p, Property) \longrightarrow Type(?p, Resource)$$
$$Type(?c, Class) \longrightarrow Type(?c, Resource)$$

Finally, the predicate in an RDF statement must be a property:

$$PropVal(?p, ?r, ?v) \longrightarrow Type(?p, Property)$$

### The *type* Property

*type* is a property:

$$Type(type, Property)$$

Note that it is equivalent to $PropVal(type, type, Property)$: the type of *type* is *Property*. *type* can be applied to resources and has a class as its value:

$$Type(?r, ?c) \longrightarrow (Type(?r, Resource) \land Type(?c, Class))$$

### The Auxiliary *FuncProp* Property

A functional property is a property that is a function: it relates a resource to at most one value. Functional properties are not a concept of RDF but are used in the axiomatization of other primitives.

The constant $FuncProp$ represents the class of all functional properties. $P$ is a functional property if, and only if, it is a property, and there are no $x$, $y_1$, and $y_2$ such that $P(x, y_1)$, $P(x, y_2)$, and $y_1 \neq y_2$.

$$Type(?p, FuncProp) \longleftrightarrow$$
$$(Type(?p, Property) \land \forall ?r \forall ?v1 \forall ?v2$$
$$(PropVal(?p, ?r, ?v1) \land PropVal(?p, ?r, ?v2) \longrightarrow ?v1 = ?v2))$$

### Reified Statements

The constant $Statement$ represents the class of all reified statements. All reified statements are resources, and $Statement$ is an instance of $Class$:

$$Type(?s, Statement) \longrightarrow Type(?s, Resource)$$
$$Type(Statement, Class)$$

A reified statement can be decomposed into the three parts of an RDF triple:

$$Type(?st, Statement) \longrightarrow$$
$$\exists ?p \exists ?r \exists ?v (PropVal(Predicate, ?st, ?p) \land$$
$$PropVal(Subject, ?st, ?r) \land PropVal(Object, ?st, ?v))$$

$Subject$, $Predicate$, and $Object$ are functional properties, that is, every statement has exactly one subject, one predicate and one object:

$Type(Subject, FuncProp)$

$Type(Predicate, FuncProp)$

$Type(Object, FuncProp)$

Their typing information is

$PropVal(Subject, ?st, ?r) \longrightarrow$
$(Type(?st, Statement) \wedge Type(?r, Resource))$

$PropVal(Predicate, ?st, ?p) \longrightarrow$
$(Type(?st, Statement) \wedge Type(?p, Property))$

$PropVal(Object, ?st, ?v) \longrightarrow$
$(Type(?st, Statement) \wedge (Type(?v, Resource) \vee Type(?v, Literal)))$

The last axiom says, if *Object* appears as the property in an RDF statement, then it must apply to a reified statement and have as value either a resource or a literal.

### Containers

All containers are resources:

$Type(?c, Container) \longrightarrow Type(?c, Resource)$

Containers are lists:

$Type(?c, Container) \longrightarrow list(?c)$

Containers are bags or sequences or alternatives:

$Type(?c, Container) \longleftrightarrow$
$(Type(?c, Bag) \vee Type(?c, Seq) \vee Type(?c, Alt))$

Bags and sequences are disjoint:

$\neg(Type(?x, Bag) \wedge Type(?x, Seq))$

For every natural number $n > 0$, there is the selector $\_n$, which selects the $n$th element of a container. It is a functional property

$Type(\_n, FuncProp)$

and applies to containers only:

$PropVal(\_n, ?c, ?o) \longrightarrow Type(?c, Container)$

### 3.7.4    RDF Schema

**Subclasses and Subproperties**

`subClassOf` is a property:

$$Type(subClassOf, Property)$$

If a class $C$ is a subclass of a class $C'$, then all instances of $C$ are also instances of $C'$:

$$PropVal(subClassOf, ?c, ?c') \longleftarrow$$
$$(Type(?c, Class) \land Type(?c', Class) \land$$
$$\forall ?x (Type(?x, ?c) \longrightarrow Type(?x, ?c')))$$

Similarly for `subPropertyOf`: $P$ is a subproperty of $P'$ if $P'(x, y)$ whenever $P(x, y)$:

$$Type(subPropertyOf, Property)$$

$$PropVal(subPropertyOf, ?p, ?p') \longleftrightarrow$$
$$(Type(?p, Property) \land Type(?p', Property) \land$$
$$\forall ?r \forall ?v (PropVal(?p, ?r, ?v) \longrightarrow PropVal(?p', ?r, ?v)))$$

**Constraints**

Every constraint resource is a resource:

$$PropVal(subClassOf, ConstraintResource, Resource)$$

Constraint properties are all properties that are also constraint resources:

$$Type(?cp, ConstraintProperty) \longleftrightarrow$$

$$(Type(?cp, ConstraintResource) \land Type(?cp, Property))$$

`domain` and `range` are constraint properties:

$$Type(domain, ConstraintProperty)$$
$$Type(range, ConstraintProperty)$$

`domain` and `range` define the domain, respectively range, of a property. Recall that the domain of a property $P$ is the set of all objects to which $P$ applies. If the domain of $P$ is $D$, then for every $P(x, y)$, $x \in D$.

$$PropVal(domain, ?p, ?d) \longrightarrow$$
$$\forall ?x \forall ?y (PropVal(?p, ?x, ?y) \longrightarrow Type(?x, ?d))$$

The range of a property $P$ is the set of all values $P$ can take. If the range of $P$ is $R$, then for every $P(x, y)$, $y \in R$.

$$PropVal(range, ?p, ?r) \longrightarrow$$
$$\forall ?x \forall ?y (PropVal(?p, ?x, ?y) \longrightarrow Type(?y, ?r))$$

Formulas that can be inferred from the precedings ones:

$$PropVal(domain, range, Property)$$

$$PropVal(range, range, Class)$$

$$PropVal(domain, domain, Property)$$

$$PropVal(range, domain, Class)$$

Thus we have formalized the semantics of RDF and RDFS. An agent equipped with this knowledge is able to draw interesting conclusions. For example, given that the domain of *teaches* is *academicStaffMember*, that *academicStaffMember* is a subclass of *staffMembers*, and that *teaches(DB, DiMa)*, the agent can automatically deduce *staffMember(DB)* using the predicate logic semantics or one of the predicate logic proof systems.

## 3.8   A Direct Inference System for RDF and RDFS

As stated above, the axiomatic semantics detailed in section 3.7 can be used for automated reasoning with RDF and RDF Schema. However, it requires a first-order logic proof system to do so. This is a very heavy requirement and also one that is unlikely to scale when millions of statements are involved (e.g. millions of statements of the form $Type(?r, ?c)$).

For this reason, RDF has also been given a semantics (and an inference systems that is sound and complete for this semantics) directly in terms of RDF triples instead of restating RDF in terms of first-order logic, as was done in the axiomatic semantics of section 3.7.

This inference system consists of rules of the form

| IF | E contains certain triples |
|---|---|
| THEN | add to E certain additional triples |

(where E is an arbitrary set of RDF triples).

Without repeating the entire set of inference rules (which can be found in the official RDF documents), we give here a few basic examples:

IF        E contains the triple $(?x, ?p, ?y)$
THEN    E also contains the triple $(?p, \texttt{rdf : type}, \texttt{rdf : property})$

This states that any resource $?p$ that is used in the property position of a triple can be inferred to be a member of the class $\texttt{rdf:property}$.

A somewhat more interesting example is the following rule:

IF        E contains the triples $(?u, \texttt{rdfs : subClassOf}, ?v)$
            and $(?v, \texttt{rdfs : subclassOf}, ?w)$
THEN    E also contains the triple $(?u, \texttt{rdfs : subClassOf}, ?w)$

which encodes the transitivity of the subclass relation.

Closely related is the rule

IF        E contains the triples $(?x, \texttt{rdf : type}, ?u)$
            and $(?u, \texttt{rdfs : subClassOf}, ?v)$
THEN    E also contains the triple $(?x, \texttt{rdf : type}, ?v)$

which is the essential definition of the meaning of $\texttt{rdfs:subClassOf}$.

A final example often comes as a surprise to people first looking at RDF Schema:

IF        E contains the triples $(?x, ?p, ?y)$
            and $(?p, \texttt{rdfs : range}, ?u)$
THEN    E also contains the triple $(?y, \texttt{rdf : type}, ?u)$

This rule states that any resource $?y$ which appears as the value of a property $?p$ can be inferred to be a member of the range of $?p$. This shows that range definitions in RDF Schema are not used to *restrict* the range of a property, but rather to *infer* the membership of the range.

The total set of these closure rules is no larger than a few dozen and can be efficiently implemented without sophisticated theorem-proving technology.

## 3.9    Querying in RQL

In this section we will introduce a query language for RDF. Before doing so, we have to say why we need a new query language instead of using an XML query language. The answer is that XML is located at a lower level of abstraction than RDF. This fact would lead to complications if we were querying RDF documents with an XML-based language. Let us illustrate this point.

As we have already seen, there are various ways of syntactically representing an RDF statement in XML. For example, suppose we wish to retrieve the titles of all lecturers. The description of a particular lecturer might look like this:

```
<rdf:Description rdf:about="949318">
 <rdf:type rdf:resource="&uni;lecturer"/>
 <uni:name>David Billington</uni:name>
 <uni:title>Associate Professor</uni:title>
</rdf:Description>
```

An appropriate Xpath query is

```
/rdf:Description[rdf:type=
   "http://www.mydomain.org/uni-ns#lecturer"]/uni:title
```

But we could have written the same description as follows:

```
<uni:lecturer rdf:about="949318">
 <uni:name>David Billington</uni:name>
 <uni:title>Associate Professor</uni:title>
</uni:lecturer>
```

Now the previous XPath query does not work; we have to write

```
//uni:lecturer/uni:title
```

instead. And a third possible representation of the same description is

```
<uni:lecturer rdf:about="949318"
              uni:name="David Billington"
              uni:title="Associate Professor"/>
```

For this syntactic variation, yet another XPath query must be provided:

```
//uni:lecturer/@uni:title
```

Since each description of an individual lecturer may have any of these equivalent forms, we must write different XPath queries.

A better way is, of course, to write queries at the level of RDF. An appropriate query language must understand RDF, that is, it must understand not only the syntax but also the data model of RDF and the semantics of RDF vocabulary.

In addition, a query language should also understand the semantics of RDF Schema. For example, given the information

```
<uni:lecturer rdf:about="949352">
 <uni:name>Grigoris Antoniou</uni:name>
</uni:lecturer>

<uni:professor rdf:about="949318">
 <uni:name>David Billington</uni:name>
</uni:professor>

<rdfs:Class rdf:about="&uni;professor">
 <rdfs:subClassOf rdf:resource="&uni;lecturer"/>
</rdfs:Class>
```

a query for the names of all lecturers should return both Grigoris Antoniou and David Billington.

At the time of writing (mid 2003), there is no standardization of query languages for RDF and RDFS, neither de jure by W3C, nor de facto by the community. In our discussion we have chosen to discuss RQL because it illustrates a number of features that will be part of any reasonable query language for RDF and RDFS, such as path expressions and schema awareness. However, other query languages exist (e.g., RDQL), and even RQL itself is subject to change.

### 3.9.1   Basic Queries

The query Class retrieves all classes, and the query Property retrieves all properties. To retrieve the instances of a class, for example, course, we write

```
course
```

This query will return all instances of the subclasses of course, too, which is perfectly correct. But if we do not wish to retrieve inherited instances, then we have to write

```
^course
```

The resources and values of triples with a specific property, for example, involves, are retrieved using simply the query involves. The result includes all subproperties of involves, for example, it retrieves also inherited triples from property isTaughtBy. If we do not want these additional results, then we have to write ^involves instead.

### 3.9.2 Using `select-from-where`

As in SQL,

`select` specifies the number and order of retrieved data

`from` is used to navigate through the data model

`where` imposes constraints on possible solutions

For example, to retrieve all phone numbers of staff members, we can write

```
select X,Y
from {X}phone{Y}
```

Here `X` and `Y` are variables, and `{X}phone{Y}` represents a resource-property-value triple. To retrieve all lecturers and their phone numbers, we can write

```
select X,Y
from lecturer{X}.phone{Y}
```

Here `lecturer{X}` collects all instances of the class `lecturer`, as discussed, and binds the result to the variable `X`. The second part collects all triples with predicate `phone`. But there is an *implicit join* here, in that we restrict the second query only to those triples, the resource of which is in the variable `X`; in our example, we restrict the domain of *phone* to lecturers. A dot `.` denotes the implicit join.

We demonstrate an *explicit join* by a query that retrieves the name of all courses taught by the lecturer with ID 949352.

```
select N
from course{X}.isTaughtBy{Y}, {C}name{N}
where Y="949352" and X=C
```

Apart from = there exist other *comparison operators*. For example, `X<Y` means "`X` is lower than `Y`". In case `X` and `Y` are strings, `X` comes before `Y` in the lexicographic order. If `X` and `Y` are classes, `X` is a subclass of `Y`.

### 3.9.3 Querying the Schema

RQL allows us to retrieve schema information. Schema variables have a name with prefix $ (for classes) or @ (for properties). For example,

```
select X,$X,Y,$Y
from {X:$X}phone{Y:$Y}
```

retrieves all resources and values of triples with property phone, or any of its subproperties, and their classes. Note that these classes may not coincide with the defined domain and range of phone, because they may be subclasses of the domain or range. For example, given

*phone("949352","5041")*
*type("949352",lecturer)*
*subclass(lecturer,staffMember)*
*domain(phone,staffMember)*
*range(phone,literal)*

we get

*("949352",lecturer,"5041",literal)*

although *lecturer* is not the domain of *phone*.

The domain and range of a property can be retrieved as follows:

```
select domain(@P),range(@P)
from @P
where @P=phone
```

For more details see the RQL User Manual (v2.0) (2003).

## 3.10   Summary

- RDF provides a foundation for representing and processing metadata.

- RDF has a graph-based data model. Its key concepts are resource, property, and statement. A statement is a resource-property-value triple.

- RDF has an XML-based syntax to support syntactic interoperability. XML and RDF complement each other because RDF supports semantic interoperability.

- RDF has a decentralized philosophy and allows incremental building of knowledge, and its sharing and reuse.

- RDF is domain-independent. RDF Schema provides a mechanism for describing specific domains.

- RDF Schema is a primitive ontology language. It offers certain modelling primitives with fixed meaning. Key concepts of RDF Schema are class, subclass relations, property, subproperty relations, and domain and range restrictions.

- There exist query languages for RDF and RDFS.

Some points that will be discussed in the next chapter:

- RDF Schema is quite primitive as a modelling language for the Web. Many desirable modelling primitives are missing.

- Therefore we need an ontology layer on top of RDF/RDFS.

## Suggested Reading

The following are some official online documents:

- G. Klyne and J. Carroll, eds. Resource Description Framework (RDF): Concepts and Abstract Syntax. January 23, 2003. <http://www.w3.org/TR/rdf-concepts>.

- D. Brickley and R.V. Guha, eds. RDF Vocabulary Description Language 1.0: RDF Schema, January 23, 2003. <http://www.w3.org/TR/rdf-schema>.

- P. Hayes, ed. RDF Semantics, January 23,2003. <http://www.w3.org/TR/rdf-mt/>.

- D. Beckett, ed. RDF/XML Syntax Specification, January 23, 2003. <http://www.w3.org/TR/rdf-syntax-grammar/>.

- F. Manola and E. Miller, eds. RDF Primer. <http://www.w3.org/TR/rdf-primer/>.

- R. Fikes and D. McGuinness. An Axiomatic Semantics for RDF, RDF Schema and DAML+OIL, October 2001. <http://www.daml.org/2001/03/axiomatic-semantics.html>.

- The RQL v2.0 User Manual, July 12, 2003. <http://139.91.183.30:9090/RDF/RQL/Manual.html>.

Here are some further useful readings:

- S. Decker et al. The Semantic Web: The Roles of XML and RDF. *IEEE Internet Computing* 15,3 (October 2000): 63–74.

- D. Dodds et al. *Professional XML Meta Data.* Birmingham, U.K., Wrox Press, 2001.

- J. Hjelm. *Creating the Semantic Web with RDF.* New York, Wiley, 2001.

- G. Karvounarakis, V. Christophides, D. Plexousakis, and S. Alexaki. *Querying Community Web Portals.* Technical Report, ICS-FORTH, Heraklion, Greece, November 2000. <http://139.91.183.30:9090/RDF/publications/sigmod2000.html>.

- J. Broekstra, Sesame RQL: a tutorial. <http://sesame.aduna.biz/publications/rql-tutorial.html>.

- M. Nic. RDF Tutorial - Part I: Basic Syntax and Containers. <http://www.zvon.org/xxl/RDFTutorial/General/book.html>.

An extensive list of tools and other resources is maintained at:

- <http://www.ilrt.bris.ac.uk/discovery/rdf/resources/>.

- <http://www.w3.org/RDF>

## Exercises and Projects

3.1  Read the RDFS namespace and try to understand the elements that were not presented in this chapter.

3.2  Read the manual on RQL, focusing on points not discussed here.

3.3  The RDFS specification allows more than one domain to be defined for a property and uses the union of these domains. Discuss the pros and cons of taking the union versus taking the intersection of domains.

3.4  In an older version of the RDFS specification, rdfs:subClassOf was not allowed to have cycles. Try to imagine situations where a cyclic class relationship would be beneficial. (*Hint:* Think of equivalence between classes.)

3.5  Discuss the difference between the following statements, and draw graphs to illustrate the difference:

> X supports the proposal; Y supports the proposal; Z supports the proposal. The group of X, Y, and Z supports the proposal.

Draw graphs to illustrate the difference.

3.6 Compare `rdfs:subClassOf` with type extensions in XML Schema.

3.7 Consider the formal specification of `rdf:_n` in the axiomatic semantics. Does it capture the intended meaning of `rdf:_n` as the selector of the nth element of a collection? If not, suggest a full axiomatization.

3.8 Prove the inferred formulas at the end of section 3.7 using the previous axioms.

3.9 Discuss why RDF/S does not allow logical contradictions: any RDF/S document is consistent, thus it has at least one model.

3.10 Try to map the relational database model on RDF.

3.11 Compare entity-relationship modelling to RDF.

3.12 Model part of a library in RDF Schema: books, authors, publishers, years, copies, dates, and so on. Then write some statements in RDF, and query them using RQL.

3.13 Write an ontology about geography: cities, countries, capitals, borders, states, and so on.

3.14 In chapter 2 you were asked to consider various domains and develop appropriate vocabularies for them. Try to model these domains by defining suitable classes and properties, and a conceptual model. Then write sample statements in RDF.

In the following you are asked to think about limitations of RDFS, specifically, what should actually be expressed, and whether it can be represented in RDF Schema. These limitations will be relevant in chapter 4, where we present a richer modelling language.

3.15 Consider the classes of males, and females. Name a relationship between them that should be included in an ontology.

3.16 Consider the classes of persons, males and females. Name a relationship between all three that should be included in an ontology. Which part of this relationship can be expressed in RDF Schema?

3.17   Suppose we declare Bob and Peter to be the father of Mary. Obviously there is a semantic error here. How should the semantic model make this error impossible?

3.18   What relationship exists between "is child of" and "is parent of"?

3.19   Consider the property *eats* with domain *animal* and range *animal or plant*. Suppose we define a new class *vegetarian*. Name a desirable restriction on *eats* for this class. Do you think that this restriction can be expressed in RDF Schema by using `rdfs:range`?

3.20   Evaluate some RQL queries against the RDF repositories that are available at <http://sesame.aduna.biz>.

3.21   Construct an RDF Schema vocabulary on a topic of your choice, and use the FRODO RDFSViz visualisation tool[2] to construct a class and property diagram for your vocabulary.

---

2.  <http://www.dfki.uni-kl.de/frodo/RDFSViz/>

# 4 *Web Ontology Language: OWL*

## 4.1 Introduction

The expressivity of RDF and RDF Schema that we described in the previous chapter is deliberately very limited: RDF is (roughly) limited to binary ground predicates, and RDF Schema is (roughly) limited to a subclass hierarchy and a property hierarchy, with domain and range definitions of these properties.

However, the Web Ontology Working Group of W3C[1] identified a number of characteristic use-cases for the Semantic Web that would require much more expressiveness than RDF and RDF Schema offer.

A number of research groups in both the United States and Europe had already identified the need for a more powerful ontology modeling language. This led to a joint initiative to define a richer language, called DAML+OIL[2] (the name is a join of the names of the U.S. proposal DAML-ONT,[3] and the European language OIL[4]).

DAML+OIL in turn was taken as the starting point for the W3C Web Ontology Working Group in defining OWL, the language that is aimed to be the standardized and broadly accepted ontology language of the Semantic Web.

In this chapter, we first describe the motivation for OWL in terms of its requirements, and its resulting nontrivial relation with RDF Schema. We then describe the various language elements of OWL in some detail.

---

1. <http://www.w3.org/2001/sw/WebOnt/>
2. <http://www.daml.org/2001/03/daml+oil-index.html>
3. <http://www.daml.org/2000/10/daml-ont.html>
4. <http://www.ontoknowledge.org/oil/>

### 4.1.1    Requirements for Ontology Languages

Ontology languages allow users to write explicit, formal conceptualizations of domain models. The main requirements are

| | |
|---|---|
| a well-defined syntax | efficient reasoning support |
| a formal semantics | sufficient expressive power |
| convenience of expression. | |

The importance of a *well-defined syntax* is clear, and known from the area of programming languages; it is a necessary condition for machine-processing of information. All the languages we have presented so far have a well-defined syntax. DAML+OIL and OWL build upon RDF and RDFS and have the same kind of syntax.

Of course, it is questionable whether the XML-based RDF syntax is very user-friendly; there are alternatives better suitable for human users (for example, see the OIL syntax). However, this drawback is not very significant because ultimately users will be developing their own ontologies using authoring tools, or more generally, *ontology development tools*, instead of writing them directly in DAML+OIL or OWL.

A *formal semantics* describes the meaning of knowledge precisely. *Precisely* here means that the semantics does not refer to subjective intuitions, nor is it open to different interpretations by different people (or machines). The importance of a formal semantics is well-established in the domain of mathematical logic, for instance.

One use of a formal semantics is to allow people to reason about the knowledge. For ontological knowledge, we may reason about

- Class membership. If $x$ is an instance of a class $C$, and $C$ is a subclass of $D$, then we can infer that $x$ is an instance of $D$.

- Equivalence of classes. If class $A$ is equivalent to class $B$, and class $B$ is equivalent to class $C$, then $A$ is equivalent to $C$, too.

- Consistency. Suppose we have declared $x$ to be an instance of the class $A$ and that $A$ is a subclass of $B \cap C$, $A$ is a subclass of $D$, and $B$ and $D$ are disjoint. Then we have an inconsistency because $A$ should be empty, but has the instance $x$. This is an indication of an error in the ontology.

- Classification. If we have declared that certain property-value pairs are a sufficient condition for membership in a class $A$, then if an individual $x$ satisfies such conditions, we can conclude that $x$ must be an instance of $A$.

Semantics is a prerequisite for *reasoning support*. Derivations such as the preceding ones can be made mechanically instead of being made by hand. Reasoning support is important because it allows one to

- check the consistency of the ontology and the knowledge

- check for unintended relationships between classes

- automatically classify instances in classes

Automated reasoning support allows one to check many more cases than could be checked manually. Checks like the precedings ones are valuable for designing large ontologies, where multiple authors are involved, and for integrating and sharing ontologies from various sources.

A Formal semantics and reasoning support are usually provided by mapping an ontology language to a known logical formalism, and by using automated reasoners that already exist for those formalisms. OWL is (partially) mapped on a description logic, and makes use of existing reasoners such as FaCT and RACER. Description logics are a subset of predicate logic for which efficient reasoning support is possible.

### 4.1.2   Limitations of the Expressive Power of RDF Schema

RDF and RDFS allow the representation of *some* ontological knowledge. The main modeling primitives of RDF/RDFS concern the organization of vocabularies in typed hierarchies: subclass and subproperty relationships, domain and range restrictions, and instances of classes. However, a number of other features are missing. Here we list a few:

- Local scope of properties. `rdfs:range` defines the range of a property, say `eats`, for all classes. Thus in RDF Schema we cannot declare range restrictions that apply to some classes only. For example, we cannot say that cows eat only plants, while other animals may eat meat, too.

- Disjointness of classes. Sometimes we wish to say that classes are disjoint. For example, `male` and `female` are disjoint. But in RDF Schema we can only state subclass relationships, e.g., `female` is a subclass of `person`.

- Boolean combinations of classes. Sometimes we wish to build new classes by combining other classes using union, intersection, and complement. For example, we may wish to define the class `person` to be the disjoint union of the classes `male` and `female`. RDF Schema does not allow such definitions.

- Cardinality restrictions. Sometimes we wish to place restrictions on how many distinct values a property may or must take. For example, we would like to say that a person has exactly two parents, or that a course is taught by at least one lecturer. Again, such restrictions are impossible to express in RDF Schema.

- Special characteristics of properties. Sometimes it is useful to say that a property is *transitive* (like "greater than"), *unique* (like "is mother of"), or the *inverse* of another property (like "eats" and "is eaten by").

Thus we need an ontology language that is richer than RDF Schema, a language that offers these features and more. In designing such a language one should be aware of the trade-off between expressive power and efficient reasoning support. Generally speaking, the richer the language is, the more inefficient the reasoning support becomes, often crossing the border of noncomputability. Thus we need a compromise, a language that can be supported by reasonably efficient reasoners while being sufficiently expressive to express large classes of ontologies and knowledge.

### 4.1.3   Compatibility of OWL with RDF/RDFS

Ideally, OWL would be an extension of RDF Schema, in the sense that OWL would use the RDF meaning of classes and properties ( `rdfs:Class`, `rdfs:subClassOf`, etc.) and would add language primitives to support the richer expressiveness required. Such an extension of RDF Schema would also be consistent with the layered architecture of the Semantic Web (see figure 1.3).

Unfortunately, simply extending RDF Schema would work against obtaining expressive power and efficient reasoning. RDF Schema has some very powerful modeling primitives (see figure 3.8). Constructions such as `rdfs:Class` (the class of all classes) and `rdf:Property` (the class of all properties) are very expressive and would lead to uncontrollable computational properties if the logic were extended with such expressive primitives.

### 4.1.4 Three Species of OWL

The full set of requirements for an ontology language that seem unobtainable: efficient reasoning support and convenience of expression for a language as powerful as a combination of RDF Schema with a full logic.

Indeed, these requirements have prompted W3C's Web Ontology Working Group to define OWL as three different sublanguages, each geared toward fulfilling different aspects of this full set of requirements.

#### OWL Full

The entire language is called OWL Full and uses all the OWL languages primitives. It also allows the combination of these primitives in arbitrary ways with RDF and RDF Schema. This includes the possibility (also present in RDF) of changing the meaning of the predefined (RDF or OWL) primitives by applying the language primitives to each other. For example, in OWL Full, we could impose a cardinality constraint on the class of all classes, essentially limiting the number of classes that can be described in any ontology.

The advantage of OWL Full is that it is fully upward-compatible with RDF, both syntactically and semantically: any legal RDF document is also a legal OWL Full document, and any valid RDF/RDF Schema conclusion is also a valid OWL Full conclusion. The disadvantage of OWL Full is that the language has become so powerful as to be undecidable, dashing any hope of complete (or efficient) reasoning support.

#### OWL DL

In order to regain computational efficiency, OWL DL (short for Description Logic) is a sublanguage of OWL Full that restricts how the constructors from OWL and RDF may be used: essentially application of OWL's constructor's to each other is disallowed, thus ensuring that the language corresponds to a well studied description logic.

The advantage of this is that it permits efficient reasoning support. The disadvantage is that we lose full compatibility with RDF: an RDF document will in general have to be extended in some ways and restricted in others before it is a legal OWL DL document. Every legal OWL DL document is a legal RDF document.

**OWL Lite**

An even further restriction limits OWL DL to a subset of the language constructors. For example, OWL Lite excludes enumerated classes, disjointness statements, and arbitrary cardinality.

The advantage of this is a language that is both easier to grasp (for users) and easier to implement (for tool builders). The disadvantage is of course a restricted expressivity.

Ontology developers adopting OWL should consider which sublanguage best suits their needs. The choice between OWL Lite and OWL DL depends on the extent to which users require the more expressive constructs provided by OWL DL and OWL Full. The choice between OWL DL and OWL Full mainly depends on the extent to which users require the metamodeling facilities of RDF Schema (e.g., defining classes of classes, or attaching properties to classes). When using OWL Full as compared to OWL DL, reasoning support is less predictable because complete OWL Full implementations will be impossible.

There are strict notions of upward compatibility between these three sublanguages:

- Every legal OWL Lite ontology is a legal OWL DL ontology.

- Every legal OWL DL ontology is a legal OWL Full ontology.

- Every valid OWL Lite conclusion is a valid OWL DL conclusion.

- Every valid OWL DL conclusion is a valid OWL Full conclusion.

OWL still uses RDF and RDF Schema to a large extent:

- All varieties of OWL use RDF for their syntax.

- Instances are declared as in RDF, using RDF descriptions and typing information.

- OWL constructors like `owl:Class`, and `owl:DatatypeProperty`, and `owl:ObjectProperty` are specialisations of their RDF counterparts.

Figure 4.1 shows the subclass relationships between some modeling primitives of OWL and RDF/RDFS.

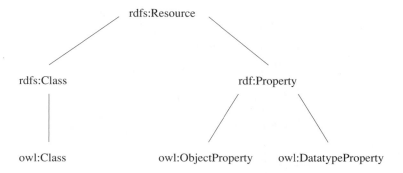

**Figure 4.1**   Subclass relationships between OWL and RDF/RDFS

One of the main motivations behind the layered architecture of the Semantic Web (see Figure 1.3) is a hope for downward compatibility with corresponding reuse of software across the various layers. However, the advantage of full downward compatibility for OWL (that any OWL-aware processor will also provide correct interpretations of any RDF Schema document) is only achieved for OWL Full, at the cost of computational intractability.

In this chapter, section 4.2 presents OWL in some detail, and section 4.3 illustrates the language with examples.

Part of the OWL definition can be written in OWL itself. as shown in section 4.4. Section 4.5 discusses some representational requirements not handled by OWL, which may be the subject of future extensions.

## 4.2   The OWL Language

### 4.2.1   Syntax

OWL builds on RDF and RDF Schema and uses RDF's XML-based syntax. Since this is the primary syntax for OWL, we use it here, but RDF/XML does not provide a very readable syntax. Because of this, other syntactic forms for OWL have also been defined:

- An XML-based syntax[5] that does not follow the RDF conventions and is thus more easily read by human users.

---

5.  defined in <http://www.w3.org/TR/owl-xmlsyntax/>

- An abstract syntax, used in the language specification document[6], that is much more compact and readable then either the XML syntax or the RDF/XML syntax. Appendix A lists all the RDF/XML code in this chapter in this abstract syntax.

- a graphic syntax based on the conventions of UML (Unified Modeling Language), which is widely used, and is thus an easy way for people to become familiar with OWL.

### 4.2.2  Header

OWL documents are usually called *OWL ontologies* and are RDF documents. The root element of an OWL ontology is an `rdf:RDF` element, which also specifies a number of namespaces:

```
<rdf:RDF
    xmlns:owl ="http://www.w3.org/2002/07/owl#"
    xmlns:rdf ="http://www.w3.org/1999/02/22-rdf-syntax-ns#"
    xmlns:rdfs="http://www.w3.org/2000/01/rdf-schema#"
    xmlns:xsd ="http://www.w3.org/2001/XMLSchema#">
```

An OWL ontology may start with a collection of assertions for housekeeping purposes. These assertions are grouped under an `owl:Ontology` element, which contains comments, version control, and inclusion of other ontologies. For example:

```
<owl:Ontology rdf:about="">
  <rdfs:comment>An example OWL ontology</rdfs:comment>
  <owl:priorVersion
        rdf:resource="http://www.mydomain.org/uni-ns-old"/>
  <owl:imports
        rdf:resource="http://www.mydomain.org/persons"/>
  <rdfs:label>University Ontology</rdfs:label>
</owl:Ontology>
```

Only one of these assertions has any consequences for the logical meaning of the ontology: `owl:imports`, which lists other ontologies whose content is assumed to be part of the current ontology. Note that while namespaces are used for disambiguation, imported ontologies provide definitions that can

---

6. <http://www.w3.org/TR/owl-semantics/>

be used. Usually there will be an import element for each namespace used, but it is possible to import additional ontologies, for example, ontologies that provide definitions without introducing any new names.

Also note that owl:imports is a transitive property: if ontology $A$ imports ontology $B$, and ontology $B$ imports ontology $C$, then ontology $A$ also imports ontology $C$.

### 4.2.3   Class Elements

Classes are defined using an owl:Class element.[7]  For example, we can define a class associateProfessor as follows:

```
<owl:Class rdf:ID="associateProfessor">
  <rdfs:subClassOf rdf:resource="#academicStaffMember"/>
</owl:Class>
```

We can also say that this class is disjoint from the assistantProfessor and professor classes using owl:disjointWith elements. These elements can be included in the preceding definition, or added by referring to the ID using rdf:about. This mechanism is inherited from RDF.

```
<owl:Class rdf:about="#associateProfessor">
  <owl:disjointWith rdf:resource="#professor"/>
  <owl:disjointWith rdf:resource="#assistantProfessor"/>
</owl:Class>
```

Equivalence of classes can be defined using an owl:equivalentClass element:

```
<owl:Class rdf:ID="faculty">
  <owl:equivalentClass rdf:resource="#academicStaffMember"/>
</owl:Class>
```

Finally, there are two predefined classes, owl:Thing and owl:Nothing. The former is the most general class, which contains everything (everything is a thing), and the latter is the empty class. Thus every class is a subclass of owl:Thing and a superclass of owl:Nothing.

---

7. owl:Class is a subclass of rdfs:Class.

### 4.2.4   Property Elements

In OWL there are two kinds of properties:

- Object properties, which relate objects to other objects. Examples are `is-TaughtBy` and `supervises`.

- Data type properties, which relate objects to datatype values. Examples are `phone`, `title` and `age` etc. OWL does not have any predefined data types, nor does it provide special definition facilities. Instead, it allows one to use XML Schema data types, thus making use of the layered architecture of the Semantic Web

Here is an example of a datatype property:

```
<owl:DatatypeProperty rdf:ID="age">
  <rdfs:range rdf:resource="http://www.w3.org/2001/XMLSchema
  #nonNegativeInteger"/>
</owl:DatatypeProperty>
```

User-defined data types will usually be collected in an XML schema and then used in an OWL ontology.

Here is an example of an object property:

```
<owl:ObjectProperty rdf:ID="isTaughtBy">
  <rdfs:domain rdf:resource="#course"/>
  <rdfs:range rdf:resource="#academicStaffMember"/>
  <rdfs:subPropertyOf rdf:resource="#involves"/>
</owl:ObjectProperty>
```

More than one domain and range may be declared. In this case the intersection of the domains, respectively ranges, is taken.

OWL allows us to relate "inverse properties". A typical example is the pair `isTaughtBy` and `teaches`:

```
<owl:ObjectProperty rdf:ID="teaches">
  <rdfs:range rdf:resource="#course"/>
  <rdfs:domain rdf:resource="#academicStaffMember"/>
  <owl:inverseOf rdf:resource="#isTaughtBy"/>
</owl:ObjectProperty>
```

Figure 4.2 illustrates the relationship between a property and its inverse. Actually domain and range can be inherited from the inverse property (interchange domain with range).

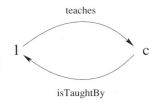

**Figure 4.2** Inverse properties

Equivalence of properties can be defined through the use of the element
`owl:equivalentProperty`.

```
<owl:ObjectProperty rdf:ID="lecturesIn">
  <owl:equivalentProperty rdf:resource="#teaches"/>
</owl:ObjectProperty>
```

### 4.2.5 Property Restrictions

With `rdfs:subClassOf` we can specify a class $C$ to be subclass of another
class $C'$; then every instance of $C$ is also an instance of $C'$.

Suppose we wish to declare, instead, that the class $C$ satisfies certain conditions, that is, all instances of $C$ satisfy the conditions. This is equivalent to
saying that $C$ is subclass of a class $C'$, where $C'$ collects all objects that satisfy
the conditions. That is exactly how it is done in OWL. Note that, in general,
$C'$ can remain anonymous.

The following element requires first-year courses to be taught by professors only (according to a questionable view, older and more senior academics
are better at teaching):

```
<owl:Class rdf:about="#firstYearCourse">
  <rdfs:subClassOf>
    <owl:Restriction>
      <owl:onProperty rdf:resource="#isTaughtBy"/>
      <owl:allValuesFrom rdf:resource="#Professor"/>
    </owl:Restriction>
  </rdfs:subClassOf>
</owl:Class>
```

`owl:allValuesFrom` is used to specify the class of possible values the
property specified by `owl:onProperty` can take (in other words, all values

of the property must come from this class). In our example, only professors are allowed as values of the property isTaughtBy.

We can declare that mathematics courses are taught by David Billington as follows:

```
<owl:Class rdf:about="#mathCourse">
  <rdfs:subClassOf>
    <owl:Restriction>
      <owl:onProperty rdf:resource="#isTaughtBy"/>
      <owl:hasValue rdf:resource="#949352"/>
    </owl:Restriction>
  </rdfs:subClassOf>
</owl:Class>
```

owl:hasValue states a specific value that the property specified by owl:onProperty must have.

And we can declare that all academic staff members must teach at least one undergraduate course:

```
<owl:Class rdf:about="#academicStaffMember">
  <rdfs:subClassOf>
    <owl:Restriction>
      <owl:onProperty rdf:resource="#teaches"/>
      <owl:someValuesFrom
          rdf:resource="#undergraduateCourse"/>
    </owl:Restriction>
  </rdfs:subClassOf>
</owl:Class>
```

Let us compare owl:allValuesFrom and owl:someValuesFrom. The example using the former requires *every* person who teaches an instance of the class, a first-year subject, to be a professor. In terms of logic, we have a *universal quantification*.

The example using the latter requires that *there exists* an undergraduate course taught by an instance of the class, an academic staff member. It is still possible that the same academic teaches postgraduate courses in addition. In terms of logic, we have an *existential quantification*.

In general, an owl:Restriction element contains an owl:onProperty element and one or more restriction declarations. One type of restriction declarations defines restrictions on the kinds of values the property can take: owl:allValuesFrom, owl:hasValue, and owl:someValuesFrom. Another type defines cardinality restrictions. For example, we can require every course to be taught by at least someone:

```
<owl:Class rdf:about="#course">
 <rdfs:subClassOf>
  <owl:Restriction>
   <owl:onProperty rdf:resource="#isTaughtBy"/>
   <owl:minCardinality
        rdf:datatype="&xsd;nonNegativeInteger">
     1
   </owl:minCardinality>
  </owl:Restriction>
 </rdfs:subClassOf>
</owl:Class>
```

Notice that we had to specify that the literal "1" is to be interpreted as non-NegativeInteger (instead of, say, a string), and that we used the xsd namespace declaration made in the header element to refer to the XML Schema document.

Or we might specify that, for practical reasons, a department must have at least ten and at most thirty members:

```
<owl:Class rdf:about="#department">
 <rdfs:subClassOf>
  <owl:Restriction>
   <owl:onProperty rdf:resource="#hasMember"/>
    <owl:minCardinality
        rdf:datatype="&xsd;nonNegativeInteger">
     10
   </owl:minCardinality>
  </owl:Restriction>
 </rdfs:subClassOf>
 <rdfs:subClassOf>
  <owl:Restriction>
   <owl:onProperty rdf:resource="#hasMember"/>
    <owl:maxCardinality
        rdf:datatype="&xsd;nonNegativeInteger">
     30
   </owl:maxCardinality>
  </owl:Restriction>
 </rdfs:subClassOf>
</owl:Class>
```

It is possible to specify a precise number, for example, a Ph.D. student must have exactly two supervisors. This can be achieved by using the same number in `owl:minCardinality` and `owl:maxCardinality`. For convenience, OWL offers also `owl:cardinality`.

We conclude by noting that `owl:Restriction` defines an anonymous class which has no ID, is not defined by `owl:Class`, and has only local scope: it can only be used in the one place where the restriction appears. When we talk about classes, please keep in mind the twofold meaning: classes that are defined by `owl:Class` with an ID, and local anonymous classes as collections of objects that satisfy certain restriction conditions, or as combinations of other classes. The latter are sometimes called *class expressions*.

### 4.2.6   Special Properties

Some properties of property elements can be defined directly:

`owl:TransitiveProperty`  defines a transitive property, such as "has better grade than", "is taller than", or "is ancestor of".

`owl:SymmetricProperty`  defines a symmetric property, such as "has same grade as" or "is sibling of".

`owl:FunctionalProperty`  defines a property that has at most one value for each object, such as "age", "height", or "directSupervisor".

`owl:InverseFunctionalProperty`  defines a property for which two different objects cannot have the same value, for example, the property "isTheSocialSecurityNumberfor" (a social security number is assigned to one person only).

An example of the syntactic forms for these is:

```
<owl:ObjectProperty rdf:ID="hasSameGradeAs">
  <rdf:type rdf:resource="&owl;TransitiveProperty" />
  <rdf:type rdf:resource="&owl;SymmetricProperty" />
  <rdfs:domain rdf:resource="#student" />
  <rdfs:range rdf:resource="#student" />
</owl:ObjectProperty>
```

### 4.2.7  Boolean Combinations

It is possible to talk about Boolean combinations (union, intersection, complement) of classes (be they defined by `owl:Class` or by class expressions). For example, we can say that courses and staff members are disjoint as follows:

```
<owl:Class rdf:about="#course">
  <rdfs:subClassOf>
    <owl:Class>
      <owl:complementOf rdf:resource="#staffMember"/>
    </owl:Class>
  </rdfs:subClassOf>
</owl:Class>
```

This says that every course is an instance of the complement of staff members, that is, no course is a staff member. Note that this statement could also have been expressed using `owl:disjointWith`.

The union of classes is built using `owl:unionOf`:

```
<owl:Class rdf:ID="peopleAtUni">
  <owl:unionOf rdf:parseType="Collection">
    <owl:Class rdf:about="#staffMember"/>
    <owl:Class rdf:about="#student"/>
  </owl:unionOf>
</owl:Class>
```

This does not say that the new class is a subclass of the union, but rather that the new class is *equal* to the union. In other words, we have stated an *equivalence of classes*. Also, we did not specify that the two classes must be disjoint: it is possible for a staff member to also be a student.

Intersection is stated with `owl:intersectionOf`:

```
<owl:Class rdf:ID="facultyInCS">
  <owl:intersectionOf rdf:parseType="Collection">
    <owl:Class rdf:about="#faculty"/>
    <owl:Restriction>
      <owl:onProperty rdf:resource="#belongsTo"/>
      <owl:hasValue rdf:resource="#CSDepartment"/>
    </owl:Restriction>
  </owl:intersectionOf>
</owl:Class>
```

Note that we have built the intersection of two classes, one of which was defined anonymously: the class of all objects belonging to the CS department. This class is intersected with `faculty` to give us the faculty in the CS department.

Boolean combinations can be nested arbitrarily. The following example defines administrative staff to be those staff members that are neither faculty nor technical support staff:

```
<owl:Class rdf:ID="adminStaff">
 <owl:intersectionOf rdf:parseType="Collection">
  <owl:Class rdf:about="#staffMember"/>
  <owl:Class>
   <owl:complementOf>
    <owl:Class>
     <owl:unionOf rdf:parseType="Collection">
      <owl:Class rdf:about="#faculty"/>
      <owl:Class rdf:about="#techSupportStaff"/>
     </owl:unionOf>
    </owl:Class>
   </owl:complementOf>
  </owl:Class>
 </owl:intersectionOf>
</owl:Class>
```

### 4.2.8   Enumerations

An enumeration is an `owl:oneOf` element, used to define a class by listing all its elements:

```
<owl:Class rdf:ID="weekdays">
 <owl:oneOf rdf:parseType="Collection">
  <owl:Thing rdf:about="#Monday"/>
  <owl:Thing rdf:about="#Tuesday"/>
  <owl:Thing rdf:about="#Wednesday"/>
  <owl:Thing rdf:about="#Thursday"/>
  <owl:Thing rdf:about="#Friday"/>
  <owl:Thing rdf:about="#Saturday"/>
  <owl:Thing rdf:about="#Sunday"/>
 </owl:oneOf>
</owl:Class>
```

### 4.2.9   Instances

Instances of classes are declared as in RDF:

```
<rdf:Description rdf:ID="949352">
 <rdf:type rdf:resource="#academicStaffMember"/>
</rdf:Description>
```

or equivalently

```
<academicStaffMember rdf:ID="949352"/>
```

We can also provide further details, such as

```
<academicStaffMember rdf:ID="949352">
 <uni:age rdf:datatype="&xsd;integer">39</uni:age>
</academicStaffMember>
```

Unlike typical database systems, OWL does not adopt the *unique-names as-sumption*; just because two instances have a different name or ID does not imply that they are different individuals. For example, if we state that each course is taught by at most one staff member

```
<owl:ObjectProperty rdf:ID="isTaughtBy">
 <rdf:type rdf:resource="&owl;FunctionalProperty" />
</owl:ObjectProperty>
```

and we subsequently state that a given course is taught by two staff members

```
<course rdf:ID="CIT1111">
 <isTaughtBy rdf:resource="#949318"/>
 <isTaughtBy rdf:resource="#949352"/>
</course>
```

this does *not* cause an OWL reasoner to flag an error. After all, the system could validly infer that the resources "949318" and "949352" are appar-ently equal. To ensure that different individuals are indeed recognized as such, we must explicitly assert their inequality:

```
<lecturer rdf:ID="949318">
 <owl:differentFrom rdf:resource="#949352"/>
</lecturer>
```

Because such inequality statements occur frequently, and the required num-ber of such statements would explode if we wanted to state the inequality of a large number of individuals, OWL provides a shorthand notation to assert the pairwise inequality of all individuals in a given list:

```
<owl:AllDifferent>
 <owl:distinctMembers rdf:parseType="Collection">
  <lecturer rdf:about="#949318"/>
  <lecturer rdf:about="#949352"/>
  <lecturer rdf:about="#949111"/>
 </owl:distinctMembers>
</owl:AllDifferent>
```

Note that `owl:distinctMembers` can only be used in combination with `owl:allDifferent`.

### 4.2.10   Data Types

Although XML Schema provides a mechanism to construct user-defined data types (e.g., the data type of `adultAge` as all integers greater than 18, or the data type of all strings starting with a number), such derived data types cannot be used in OWL. In fact, not even all of the many built-in XML Schema data types can be used in OWL. The OWL reference document lists all the XML Schema data types that can be used, but these include the most frequently used types such as string, integer, Boolean, time, and date.

### 4.2.11   Versioning Information

We have already seen the `owl:priorVersion` statement as part of the header information to indicate earlier versions of the current ontology. This information has no formal model-theoretic semantics but can be exploited by human readers and programs alike for the purposes of ontology management.

Besides `owl:priorVersion`, OWL has three more statements to indicate further informal versioning information. None of these carry any formal meaning.

`owl:versionInfo`  generally contains a string giving information about the current version, for example RCS/CVS keywords.

`owl:backwardCompatibleWith`  contains a reference to another ontology. This identifies the specified ontology as a prior version of the containing ontology and further indicates that it is backward-compatible with it. In particular, this indicates that all identifiers from the previous version have the same intended interpretations in the new version. Thus, it is a hint to document authors that they can safely change their documents to commit to the new version (by simply updating namespace declarations and `owl:imports` statements to refer to the URL of the new version).

`owl:incompatibleWith,` on the other hand, indicates that the containing ontology is a later version of the referenced ontology but is not backward-compatible with it. Essentially, this is for use by ontology authors who want to be explicit that documents cannot upgrade to use the new version without checking whether changes are required.

### 4.2.12   Layering of OWL

Now that we have discussed all the language constructors of OWL, we can completely specify which features of the language may be used in which sublanguage (OWL Full, OWL or OWL Lite).

**OWL Full**

In OWL Full, all the language constructors may be used in any combination as long as the result is legal RDF.

**OWL DL**

In order to exploit the formal underpinnings and computational tractability of Description Logics, the following constraints must be obeyed in an OWL DL ontology:

- Vocabulary partitioning. Any resource is allowed to be only a class, a data type, a data type property, an object property, an individual, a data value, or part of the built-in vocabulary, and not more than one of these. This means that, for example, a class cannot at the same time be an individual, or that a property cannot have some values from a data type and some values from a class (this would make it both a data type property and an object property).

- Explicit typing. Not only must all resources be partitioned (as prescribed in the previous constraint) but this partitioning must be stated explicitly. For example, if an ontology contains the following:

```
<owl:Class rdf:ID="C1">
  <rdfs:subClassOf rdf:about="#C2" />
</owl:Class>
```

this already entails that C2 is a class (by virtue of the range specification of `rdfs:subClassOf`). Nevertheless, an OWL DL ontology must *explicitly* state this information:

```
<owl:Class rdf:ID="C2"/>
```

- Property separation. By virtue of the first constraint, the set of object properties and data type properties are disjoint. This implies that the following can never be specified for data type properties:
  `owl:inverseOf`,
  `owl:FunctionalProperty`,
  `owl:InverseFunctionalProperty`, and
  `owl:SymmetricProperty`.

- No transitive cardinality restrictions. No cardinality restrictions may be placed on transitive properties (or their subproperties, which are of course also transitive, by implication).

- Restricted anonymous classes. Anonymous classes are only allowed to occur as the domain and range of either `owl :equivalentClass` or `owl:disjointWith`, and as the range (but not the domain) of `rdfs:subClassOf`.

**OWL Lite**

An OWL Lite ontology must be an OWL DL ontology and must further satisfy the following constraints:

- The constructors `owl:oneOf`, `owl:disjointWith`, `owl:unionOf`, `owl:complementOf` and `owl:hasValue` are not allowed.

- Cardinality statements ( minimal, maximal, and exact cardinality) can only be made on the values 0 or 1 and no longer on arbitrary non-negative integers.

- `owl:equivalentClass` statements can no longer be made between anonymous classes but only between class identifiers.

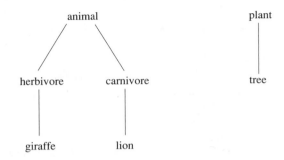

**Figure 4.3** Classes and subclasses of the African wildlife ontology

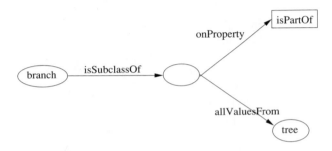

**Figure 4.4** Branches are parts of trees

## 4.3 Examples

### 4.3.1 An African Wildlife Ontology

This example shows an ontology that describes African wildlife. Figure 4.3 shows the basic classes and their subclass relationships. Note that the subclass information is only part of the information included in the ontology. The entire graph is much larger. Figure 4.4 shows the graphic representation of the statement that branches are parts of trees.

The ontology includes comments written using `rdfs:comment`.

```
<rdf:RDF
 xmlns:rdf="http://www.w3.org/1999/02/22-rdf-syntax-ns#"
 xmlns:rdfs="http://www.w3.org/2000/01/rdf-schema#"
 xmlns:owl ="http://www.w3.org/2002/07/owl#">
```

```
<owl:Ontology rdf:about="xml:base"/>

<owl:Class rdf:ID="animal">
 <rdfs:comment>Animals form a class.</rdfs:comment>
</owl:Class>

<owl:Class rdf:ID="plant">
 <rdfs:comment>
  Plants form a class disjoint from animals.
 </rdfs:comment>
 <owl:disjointWith rdf:resource="#animal"/>
</owl:Class>

<owl:Class rdf:ID="tree">
 <rdfs:comment>Trees are a type of plant.</rdfs:comment>
 <rdfs:subClassOf rdf:resource="#plant"/>
</owl:Class>

<owl:Class rdf:ID="branch">
 <rdfs:comment>Branches are parts of trees.</rdfs:comment>
 <rdfs:subClassOf>
  <owl:Restriction>
   <owl:onProperty rdf:resource="#is_part_of"/>
   <owl:allValuesFrom rdf:resource="#tree"/>
  </owl:Restriction>
 </rdfs:subClassOf>
</owl:Class>

<owl:Class rdf:ID="leaf">
<rdfs:comment>Leaves are parts of branches.</rdfs:comment>
 <rdfs:subClassOf>
  <owl:Restriction>
   <owl:onProperty rdf:resource="#is_part_of"/>
   <owl:allValuesFrom rdf:resource="#branch"/>
  </owl:Restriction>
 </rdfs:subClassOf>
</owl:Class>

<owl:Class rdf:ID="herbivore">
 <rdfs:comment>
  Herbivores are exactly those animals that eat only plants
```

```
  or parts of plants.
 </rdfs:comment>
 <owl:intersectionOf rdf:parseType="Collection">
  <owl:Class rdf:about="#animal"/>
  <owl:Restriction>
   <owl:onProperty rdf:resource="#eats"/>
   <owl:allValuesFrom>
    <owl:Class>
     <owl:unionOf rdf:parseType="Collection">
      <owl:Class rdf:about="#plant"/>
      <owl:Restriction>
       <owl:onProperty rdf:resource="#is_part_of"/>
       <owl:allValuesFrom rdf:resource="#plant"/>
      </owl:Restriction>
     </owl:unionOf>
    </owl:Class>
   </owl:allValuesFrom>
  </owl:Restriction>
 </owl:intersectionOf>
</owl:Class>

<owl:Class rdf:ID="carnivore">
 <rdfs:comment>
  Carnivores are exactly those animals that eat animals.
 </rdfs:comment>
 <owl:intersectionOf rdf:parseType="Collection">
  <owl:Class rdf:about="#animal"/>
  <owl:Restriction>
   <owl:onProperty rdf:resource="#eats"/>
   <owl:someValuesFrom rdf:resource="#animal"/>
  </owl:Restriction>
 </owl:intersectionOf>
</owl:Class>

<owl:Class rdf:ID="giraffe">
 <rdfs:comment>
  Giraffes are herbivores, and they eat only leaves.
 </rdfs:comment>
 <rdfs:subClassOf rdf:resource="#herbivore"/>
 <rdfs:subClassOf>
  <owl:Restriction>
   <owl:onProperty rdf:resource="#eats"/>
```

```
      <owl:allValuesFrom rdf:resource="#leaf"/>
    </owl:Restriction>
   </rdfs:subClassOf>
 </owl:Class>


 <owl:Class rdf:ID="lion">
  <rdfs:comment>
   Lions are animals that eat only herbivores.
  </rdfs:comment>
  <rdfs:subClassOf rdf:resource="#carnivore"/>
  <rdfs:subClassOf>
   <owl:Restriction>
    <owl:onProperty rdf:resource="#eats"/>
    <owl:allValuesFrom rdf:resource="#herbivore"/>
   </owl:Restriction>
  </rdfs:subClassOf>
 </owl:Class>

 <owl:Class rdf:ID="tasty_plant">
  <rdfs:comment>
   Tasty plants are plants that are eaten
   both by herbivores and carnivores.
  </rdfs:comment>
  <rdfs:subClassOf rdf:resource="#plant"/>
  <rdfs:subClassOf>
   <owl:Restriction>
    <owl:onProperty rdf:resource="#eaten_by"/>
    <owl:someValuesFrom>
      <owl:Class rdf:about="#herbivore"/>
    </owl:someValuesFrom>
   </owl:Restriction>
  </rdfs:subClassOf>
  <rdfs:subClassOf>
   <owl:Restriction>
    <owl:onProperty rdf:resource="#eaten_by"/>
    <owl:someValuesFrom>
      <owl:Class rdf:about="#carnivore"/>
    </owl:someValuesFrom>
   </owl:Restriction>
  </rdfs:subClassOf>
 </owl:Class>
```

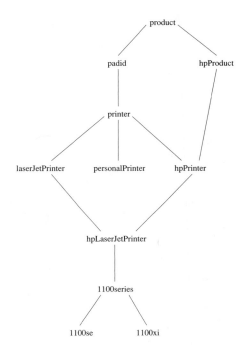

**Figure 4.5**   Classes and subclasses of the printer ontology

```
<owl:TransitiveProperty rdf:ID="is_part_of"/>

<owl:ObjectProperty rdf:ID="eats">
 <rdfs:domain rdf:resource="#animal"/>
</owl:ObjectProperty>

<owl:ObjectProperty rdf:ID="eaten_by">
 <owl:inverseOf rdf:resource="#eats"/>
</owl:ObjectProperty>

</rdf:RDF>
```

### 4.3.2   A Printer Ontology

Classes and subclass relationships in this example are shown in figure 4.5.

```
<!DOCTYPE owl [
    <!ENTITY xsd  "http://www.w3.org/2001/XMLSchema#" >
]>

<rdf:RDF
  xmlns:rdf="http://www.w3.org/1999/02/22-rdf-syntax-ns#"
  xmlns:rdfs="http://www.w3.org/2000/01/rdf-schema#"
  xmlns:xsd="http://www.w3.org/2001/XMLSchema#"
  xmlns:owl ="http://www.w3.org/2002/07/owl#"
  xmlns="http://www.cs.vu.nl/~frankh/spool/printer.owl#">

<owl:Ontology rdf:about="">
 <owl:versionInfo>
  My example version 1.2, 17 October 2002
 </owl:versionInfo>
</owl:Ontology>

<owl:Class rdf:ID="product">
 <rdfs:comment>Products form a class.</rdfs:comment>
</owl:Class>

<owl:Class rdf:ID="padid">
 <rdfs:comment>
  Printing and digital imaging devices
  form a subclass of products.
 </rdfs:comment>
 <rdfs:label>Device</rdfs:label>
 <rdfs:subClassOf rdf:resource="#product"/>
</owl:Class>

<owl:Class rdf:ID="hpProduct">
 <rdfs:comment>
  HP products are exactly those products
  that are manufactured by Hewlett Packard.
 </rdfs:comment>
 <owl:intersectionOf rdf:parseType="Collection">
  <owl:Class rdf:about="#product"/>
  <owl:Restriction>
   <owl:onProperty rdf:resource="#manufactured_by"/>
```

```
     <owl:hasValue rdf:datatype="&xsd;string">
       Hewlett Packard
     </owl:hasValue>
    </owl:Restriction>
   </owl:intersectionOf>
 </owl:Class>

 <owl:Class rdf:ID="printer">
  <rdfs:comment>
   Printers are printing and digital imaging devices.
  </rdfs:comment>
  <rdfs:subClassOf rdf:resource="#padid"/>
 </owl:Class>

 <owl:Class rdf:ID="personalPrinter">
  <rdfs:comment>
   Printers for personal use form a subclass of printers.
  </rdfs:comment>
  <rdfs:subClassOf rdf:resource="#printer"/>
 </owl:Class>

 <owl:Class rdf:ID="hpPrinter">
  <rdfs:comment>
   HP printers are  HP products and printers.
  </rdfs:comment>
  <rdfs:subClassOf rdf:resource="#printer"/>
  <rdfs:subClassOf rdf:resource="#hpProduct"/>
 </owl:Class>

 <owl:Class rdf:ID="laserJetPrinter">
  <rdfs:comment>
   Laser jet printers are exactly those
   printers that use laser jet printing technology.
  </rdfs:comment>
  <owl:intersectionOf rdf:parseType="Collection">
   <owl:Class rdf:about="#printer"/>
   <owl:Restriction>
    <owl:onProperty rdf:resource="#printingTechnology"/>
    <owl:hasValue rdf:datatype="&xsd;string">
     laser jet
    </owl:hasValue>
   </owl:Restriction>
```

```
  </owl:intersectionOf>
 </owl:Class>

 <owl:Class rdf:ID="hpLaserJetPrinter">
  <rdfs:comment>
   HP laser jet printers are HP products
   and laser jet printers.
  </rdfs:comment>
  <rdfs:subClassOf rdf:resource="#laserJetPrinter"/>
  <rdfs:subClassOf rdf:resource="#hpPrinter"/>
 </owl:Class>

 <owl:Class rdf:ID="1100series">
  <rdfs:comment>
   1100series printers are HP laser jet printers with
   8ppm printing speed and 600dpi printing resolution.
  </rdfs:comment>
  <rdfs:subClassOf rdf:resource="#hpLaserJetPrinter"/>
  <rdfs:subClassOf>
   <owl:Restriction>
    <owl:onProperty rdf:resource="#printingSpeed"/>
    <owl:hasValue rdf:datatype="&xsd;string">
     8ppm
    </owl:hasValue>
   </owl:Restriction>
  </rdfs:subClassOf>
  <rdfs:subClassOf>
   <owl:Restriction>
    <owl:onProperty rdf:resource="#printingResolution"/>
    <owl:hasValue rdf:datatype="&xsd;string">
     600dpi
    </owl:hasValue>
   </owl:Restriction>
  </rdfs:subClassOf>
 </owl:Class>

 <owl:Class rdf:ID="1100se">
  <rdfs:comment>
   1100se printers belong to the 1100 series and cost $450.
  </rdfs:comment>
  <rdfs:subClassOf rdf:resource="#1100series"/>
  <rdfs:subClassOf>
```

```
    <owl:Restriction>
     <owl:onProperty rdf:resource="#price"/>
     <owl:hasValue rdf:datatype="&xsd;integer">
      450
     </owl:hasValue>
    </owl:Restriction>
   </rdfs:subClassOf>
  </owl:Class>

  <owl:Class rdf:ID="1100xi">
   <rdfs:comment>
     1100xi printers belong to the 1100 series and cost $350.
   </rdfs:comment>
   <rdfs:subClassOf rdf:resource="#1100series"/>
   <rdfs:subClassOf>
    <owl:Restriction>
     <owl:onProperty rdf:resource="#price"/>
     <owl:hasValue rdf:datatype="&xsd;integer">
      350
     </owl:hasValue>
    </owl:Restriction>
   </rdfs:subClassOf>
  </owl:Class>

  <owl:DatatypeProperty rdf:ID="manufactured_by">
   <rdfs:domain rdf:resource="#product"/>
   <rdfs:range rdf:resource="&xsd;string"/>
  </owl:DatatypeProperty>

  <owl:DatatypeProperty rdf:ID="price">
   <rdfs:domain rdf:resource="#product"/>
   <rdfs:range rdf:resource="&xsd;nonNegativeInteger"/>
  </owl:DatatypeProperty>

  <owl:DatatypeProperty rdf:ID="printingTechnology">
   <rdfs:domain rdf:resource="#printer"/>
   <rdfs:range rdf:resource="&xsd;string"/>
  </owl:DatatypeProperty>

  <owl:DatatypeProperty rdf:ID="printingResolution">
   <rdfs:domain rdf:resource="#printer"/>
   <rdfs:range rdf:resource="&xsd;string"/>
```

```
</owl:DatatypeProperty>

<owl:DatatypeProperty rdf:ID="printingSpeed">
 <rdfs:domain rdf:resource="#printer"/>
 <rdfs:range rdf:resource="&xsd;string"/>
</owl:DatatypeProperty>


</rdf:RDF>
```

This ontology demonstrates that siblings in a hierarchy tree need not be disjoint. For example, a personal printer may be an HP printer or a LaserJet printer, although the three classes involved are subclasses of the class of all printers.

## 4.4   OWL in OWL

Here we present a part of the definition of OWL in terms of itself. The full description is found on the Web (see Suggested Reading). In our presentation we comment on some aspects of OWL that have not been discussed so far.

### 4.4.1   Namespaces

```
<?xml version="1.0"?>
<!DOCTYPE owl [
 <!ENTITY rdf "http://www.w3.org/1999/02/22-rdf-syntax-ns#">
 <!ENTITY rdfs "http://www.w3.org/2000/01/rdf-schema#">
 <!ENTITY xsd "http://www.w3.org/2001/XMLSchema#">
 <!ENTITY owl "http://www.w3.org/2002/07/owl#"> ]>
<rdf:RDF
  xml:base ="http://www.w3.org/2002/07/owl"
  xmlns     ="&owl;"
  xmlns:owl ="&owl;"
  xmlns:rdf ="&rdf;"
  xmlns:rdfs="&rdfs;"
  xmlns:dc  ="http://purl.org/dc/elements/1.1/">
```

The URI of the current document (the OWL definition) is defined as the default namespace. Therefore, the prefix owl: will not be used in the following. Also, note the use of XML entity definitions, which allows us to abbreviate URLs appearing in attribute values.

### 4.4.2   Classes of Classes (Metaclasses)

The class of all OWL classes is itself a subclass of the class of all RDF Schema classes:

```
<rdfs:Class rdf:ID="Class">
  <rdfs:label>Class</rdfs:label>
  <rdfs:comment>The class of all OWL classes</rdfs:comment>
  <rdfs:subClassOf rdf:resource="&rdfs;Class"/>
</rdfs:Class>
```

`Thing` is the most general object class in OWL, and `Nothing` the most specific, that is, the empty object class. The following relationships hold:

$$Thing = Nothing \cup Nothing^c$$
$$Nothing = Thing^c = Nothing^c \cap Nothing^{cc} = \emptyset$$

```
<Class rdf:ID="Thing">
  <rdfs:label>Thing</rdfs:label>
  <unionOf rdf:parseType="Collection">
    <Class rdf:about="#Nothing"/>
    <Class>
      <complementOf rdf:resource="#Nothing"/>
    </Class>
  </unionOf>
</Class>

<Class rdf:ID="Nothing">
  <rdfs:label>Nothing</rdfs:label>
  <complementOf rdf:resource="#Thing"/>
</Class>
```

### 4.4.3   Class Equivalence

Class equivalence, expressed by `owl:EquivalentClass`, implies a subclass relationship and is always stated between two classes. This is analogous for `owl:EquivalentProperty`. Disjointness statements can only be stated between classes.

```
<rdf:Property rdf:ID="EquivalentClass">
  <rdfs:label>EquivalentClass</rdfs:label>
  <rdfs:subPropertyOf rdf:resource="&rdfs;subClassOf"/>
  <rdfs:domain rdf:resource="#Class"/>
```

```
    <rdfs:range rdf:resource="#Class"/>
  </rdf:Property>

  <rdf:Property rdf:ID="EquivalentProperty">
    <rdfs:label>EquivalentProperty</rdfs:label>
    <rdfs:subPropertyOf rdf:resource="&rdfs;subPropertyOf"/>
  </rdf:Property>

  <rdf:Property rdf:ID="disjointWith">
    <rdfs:label>disjointWith</rdfs:label>
    <rdfs:domain rdf:resource="#Class"/>
    <rdfs:range rdf:resource="#Class"/>
  </rdf:Property>
```

Equality and inequality can be stated between arbitrary things; in OWL Full
this statement can also be applied to classes. `owl:sameAs` is simply a synonym for `owl:sameIndividualAs`.

```
  <rdf:Property rdf:ID="sameIndividualAs">
    <rdfs:label>sameIndividualAs</rdfs:label>
    <rdfs:domain rdf:resource="#Thing"/>
    <rdfs:range rdf:resource="#Thing"/>
  </rdf:Property>

  <rdf:Property rdf:ID="differentFrom">
    <rdfs:label>differentFrom</rdfs:label>
    <rdfs:domain rdf:resource="#Thing"/>
    <rdfs:range rdf:resource="#Thing"/>
  </rdf:Property>

  <rdf:Property rdf:ID="sameAs">
    <rdfs:label>sameAs</rdfs:label>
    <EquivalentProperty rdf:resource="#sameIndividualAs"/>
  </rdf:Property>
```

`owl:distinctMembers` can only be used for `owl:AllDifferent`:

```
  <rdfs:Class rdf:ID="AllDifferent">
    <rdfs:label>AllDifferent</rdfs:label>
  </rdfs:Class>

  <rdf:Property rdf:ID="distinctMembers">
    <rdfs:label>distinctMembers</rdfs:label>
```

```
    <rdfs:domain rdf:resource="#AllDifferent"/>
    <rdfs:range rdf:resource="&rdf;List"/>
  </rdf:Property>
```

### 4.4.4   Building Classes from Other Classes

`owl:unionOf` builds a class from a list (assumed to be a list of other class expressions).

```
  <rdf:Property rdf:ID="unionOf">
    <rdfs:label>unionOf</rdfs:label>
    <rdfs:domain rdf:resource="#Class"/>
    <rdfs:range rdf:resource="&rdf;List"/>
  </rdf:Property>
```

and so do `owl:intersectionOf` and `owl:oneOf`, although for these the list is assumed to be a list of individuals. `owl:complementOf` defines a class in terms of a single other class:

```
  <rdf:Property rdf:ID="complementOf">
    <rdfs:label>complementOf</rdfs:label>
    <rdfs:domain rdf:resource="#Class"/>
    <rdfs:range rdf:resource="#Class"/>
  </rdf:Property>
```

### 4.4.5   Restricting Properties of Classes

Restrictions in OWL define the class of those objects that satisfy some attached conditions:

```
  <rdfs:Class rdf:ID="Restriction">
    <rdfs:label>Restriction</rdfs:label>
    <rdfs:subClassOf rdf:resource="#Class"/>
  </rdfs:Class>
```

All the following properties are only allowed to occur within a restriction definition, that is, their domain is `owl:Restriction`, but they differ with respect to their range:

```
  <rdf:Property rdf:ID="onProperty">
    <rdfs:label>onProperty</rdfs:label>
    <rdfs:domain rdf:resource="#Restriction"/>
```

```
    <rdfs:range rdf:resource="&rdf;Property"/>
  </rdf:Property>

  <rdf:Property rdf:ID="allValuesFrom">
    <rdfs:label>allValuesFrom</rdfs:label>
    <rdfs:domain rdf:resource="#Restriction"/>
    <rdfs:range rdf:resource="&rdfs;Class"/>
  </rdf:Property>

  <rdf:Property rdf:ID="hasValue">
    <rdfs:label>hasValue</rdfs:label>
    <rdfs:domain rdf:resource="#Restriction"/>
  </rdf:Property>

  <rdf:Property rdf:ID="minCardinality">
    <rdfs:label>minCardinality</rdfs:label>
    <rdfs:domain rdf:resource="#Restriction"/>
    <rdfs:range rdf:resource="&xsd;nonNegativeInteger"/>
  </rdf:Property>
```

`owl:maxCardinality` and `owl:cardinality` are defined analogously to `owl:minCardinality`, and `owl:someValuesFrom` is defined analogously to `owl:allValuesFrom`

It is also worth noting that `owl:onProperty` allows the restriction on an object or data type property. Therefore, the range of the restricting properties like `owl:allValuesFrom` is not `owl:Class` (object classes) but the more general `rdfs:Class`.

**Properties**

`owl:ObjectProperty` is a special case of `rdf:Property`

```
  <rdfs:Class rdf:ID="ObjectProperty">
    <rdfs:label>ObjectProperty</rdfs:label>
    <rdfs:subClassOf rdf:resource="&rdf;Property"/>
  </rdfs:Class>
```

and similarly for `owl:DatatypeProperty`.

`owl:TransitiveProperty` can only be applied to object properties

```
  <rdfs:Class rdf:ID="TransitiveProperty">
    <rdfs:label>TransitiveProperty</rdfs:label>
```

```
    <rdfs:subClassOf rdf:resource="#ObjectProperty"/>
  </rdfs:Class>
```

and similarly for symmetric, functional and inverse functional properties.
Finally, `owl:inverseOf` relates two object properties:

```
<rdf:Property rdf:ID="inverseOf">
  <rdfs:label>inverseOf</rdfs:label>
  <rdfs:domain rdf:resource="#ObjectProperty"/>
  <rdfs:range rdf:resource="#ObjectProperty"/>
</rdf:Property>
```

Although not stated in the online references, the following would also seem
to be true:

```
<TransitiveProperty rdf:ID="&rdfs;subClassOf"/>
<TransitiveProperty rdf:ID="&rdfs;subProperty/>

<TransitiveProperty rdf:ID="EquivalentClass"/>
<SymmetricProperty  rdf:ID="EquivalentClass"/>

<SymmetricProperty  rdf:ID="disjointWith"/>

<TransitiveProperty rdf:ID="EquivalentProperty"/>
<SymmetricProperty  rdf:ID="EquivalentProperty"/>

<TransitiveProperty rdf:ID="sameIndividualAs"/>
<SymmetricProperty  rdf:ID="sameIndividualAs"/>

<SymmetricProperty  rdf:ID="differentFrom"/>

<SymmetricProperty  rdf:ID="complementOf"/>
<rdf:Property       rdf:about="complementOf">
  <rdfs:subPropertyOf rdf:resource="disjointWith"/>
</rdf:Property>

<rdf:Property       rdf:about="cardinality">
  <rdfs:subPropertyOf rdf:resource="mincardinality"/>
  <rdfs:subPropertyOf rdf:resource="maxcardinality"/>
</rdf:Property>

<SymmetricProperty  rdf:ID="inverseOf"/>
```

```
<rdf:Property        rdf:about="inverseOf">
  <inverseOf rdf:resource="inverseOf"/>
</rdf:Property>
```

Although this captures some of OWL's meaning in OWL, it does not capture the entire semantics, so a separate semantic specification (as given in the OWL standard) remains necessary.

## 4.5    Future Extensions

Clearly, OWL is not the final word on ontology languages for the Semantic Web. A number of additional features have already been identified in the OWL Requirements Document, and many others are under discussion. In this section, we briefly list a few of these possible extensions and improvements to OWL.

### 4.5.1    Modules and Imports

Importing ontologies defined by others will be the norm on the Semantic Web. However, the importing facility of OWL is very trivial: it only allows importing of an *entire* ontology, specified by location. Even if one would want to use only a small portion of another ontology, one would be forced to import that entire ontology. Module-constructions in programming languages are based on a notion of information hiding: the module promises to provide some functionality to the outside world (the export clause of the module), but the importing module need not concern itself with how this functionality is achieved. It is an open research question what a corresponding notion of information hiding for ontologies would be, and how it could be used as the basis for a good import construction

### 4.5.2    Defaults

Many practical knowledge representation systems allow inherited values to be overridden by more specific classes in the hierarchy, treating the inherited values as defaults. Although this is widely used in practice, no consensus has been reached on the right formalization for the nonmonotonic behaviour of default values.

### 4.5.3 Closed-World Assumption

The semantics of OWL currently adopts the standard logical model of an open-world assumption: a statement cannot be assumed true on the basis of a failure to prove it. Clearly, on the huge and only partially knowable World Wide Web, this is the correct assumption. Nevertheless, the opposite approach (a closed-world assumption: a statement is true when its negation cannot be proved) is also useful in certain applications. The closed-world assumption is closely tied to the notion of defaults and leads to the same nonmonotonic behaviour, a reason for it not to be included in OWL.

### 4.5.4 Unique-Names Assumption

Typical database applications assume that individuals with different names are indeed different individuals. OWL follows the usual logical paradigm where this is not the case. If two individuals (or classes or properties) have different names, we may still derive by inference that they must be the same. As with the non-closed-world assumption, the non-unique-names assumption is the most plausible one to make on the World Wide Web, but as before, situations exist where the unique-names assumption is useful. More subtly, one may want to indicate portions of the ontology for which the assumption does or does not hold.

### 4.5.5 Procedural Attachment

A common concept in knowledge representation is to define the meaning of a term not through explicit definitions in the language (as is done in OWL) but by attaching a piece of code to be executed for computing the meaning of the term. Although widely used, this concept does not lend itself very well to integration in a system with a formal semantics, and it has not been included in OWL.

### 4.5.6 Rules for Property Chaining

As explained previously, for reasons of decidability OWL does currently not allow the composition of properties, but of course in many applications this is a useful operation. Even more generally, one would want to define properties as general rules (Horn or otherwise) over other properties. Such integration of rule-based knowledge representation and DL-style knowledge representation is currently an active area of research.

Some of the issues mentioned here (rules, nonmonotonicity) will be addressed in chapter 5.

## 4.6   Summary

- OWL is the proposed standard for Web ontologies. It allows us to describe the semantics of knowledge in a machine-accessible way.

- OWL builds upon RDF and RDF Schema: (XML-based) RDF syntax is used; instances are defined using RDF descriptions; and most RDFS modeling primitives are used.

- Formal semantics and reasoning support is provided through the mapping of OWL on logics. Predicate logic and description logics have been used for this purpose.

While OWL is sufficiently rich to be used in practice, extensions are in the making. They will provide further logical features, including rules.

### Suggested Reading

Here are the key references for OWL:

- D. McGuinness and F van Harmelen, eds. OWL Web Ontology Language Overview. August 18, 2003. <http://www.w3.org/TR/owl-features/>.

- M. Dean and G. Schreiber, eds. F. van Harmelen, J. Hendler, I. Horrocks, D. McGuinness, P. Patel-Schneider, L. Stein, *OWL Web Ontology Language Reference*. August 18, 2003. <http://www.w3.org/TR/owl-ref/>.

- M. Smith, C. Welty, and D. McGuinness, eds. *OWL Web Ontology Language: Guide*. August 18, 2003. <http://www.w3.org/TR/owl-guide/>.

Interesting articles related to DAML+OIL and OIL include

- J. Broekstra, M. Klein, S. Decker, D. Fensel, F. van Harmelen, and I. Horrocks, Enabling knowledge representation on the Web by Extending RDF Schema. In *Proceedings of the 10th World Wide Web Conference (WWW10)*, 2001. <http://www10.org/cdrom/papers/291/>

- D. Fensel, I. Horrocks, F. van Harmelen, D. McGuinness and P. Patel-Schneider. OIL: An Ontology Infrastructure for the Semantic Web. *IEEE Intelligent Systems* 16 March-April (2001): 38–45.
  <http://www.cs.vu.nl/ frankh/abstracts/IEEE-IS01.html>.

- D. McGuiness. Ontologies come of age. In *Spinning the Semantic Web*, ed. D. Fensel, J. Hendler, H. Lieberman and W. Wahlster. MIT Press 2003.

- P. Patel-Schneider, I. Horrocks and F. van Harmelen, Reviewing the Design of DAML+OIL: An Ontology Language for the Semantic Web, In *Proceedings of the 18th National Conference on Artificial Intelligence (AAAI02)*. 2002. <http://www.cs.vu.nl/ frankh/abstracts/AAAI02.html>.

Here are a few references regarding description logics:

- F. Baader, D. Calvanese, D. McGuinness, D. Nardi, P. Patel-Schneider, eds. *The Description Logic Handbook: Theory, Implementation and Applications*. Cambrdge: Cambridge University Press, 2002.

- E. Franconi. Description Logics Course Informaton.
  <http://www.cs.man.ac.uk/~franconi/dl/course/>.

- I. Horrocks and U. Sattler. Ontology Reasoning in the *SHOQ(D)* Description Logic. In *Proceedings of the 17th International Joint Conference on Artificial Intelligence (IJCAI-01)*. 2001, 199–204.

- I. Horrocks. Tutorial on Description Logic.
  <http://www.cs.man.ac.uk/~horrocks/Slides/IJCAR-tutorial/Print/>.

Here are two interesting Web sites:

- <http://www.w3.org/2001/sw/WebOnt/>. Information on OWL.

- <http://www.daml.org>. Information on DAML+OIL. See especially the pages /language, /ontologies and /tools.

The following are a few links related to the general notion of ontologies but quite different in nature from the content of this chapter. Thesauri are simple kinds of informal ontologies.

- <http://www.lub.lu.se/metadata/subject-help.html>. An extensive collection of pointers to thesauri.

- <http://www.topicmaps.org>. Topic maps constitute a simple ontology language in use today.

- <http://dublincore.org>. An example of an ontology used extensively in the digital library domain is the Dublin Core.

## Exercises and Projects

4.1   Read the online specification and the complete namespace of OWL, at <http://w3.org>.

4.2   Give three different ways of stating that two classes are disjoint.

4.3   Express the fact that all mathematics courses are taught by David Billington only (no other lecturer may be involved). Also express the fact that the mathematics courses are exactly the courses taught by David Billington. Is the difference clear?

4.4   Strictly speaking, the notion of `SymmetricProperty` was not needed in OWL, because it could have been expressed in terms of other language primitives. Explain how this can be done. (*Hint:* Consider the inverse, too).

4.5   Similar question for `FunctionalProperty`. Show how it can be expressed using other OWL language constructions.

4.6   Determine in general which features of OWL are necessary, and which are only convenient but can be simulated by other modeling primitives.

4.7   In the African wildlife example ontology, what problem would emerge if we replaced `owl:allValuesFrom` by `owl:someValuesFrom` in the definition of carnivores? (*Hint:* Consider the definition of tasty plants).

4.8   State the relationship between the concepts
`FunctionalProperty`,
`InverseFunctionalProperty`, and
`Inverseof`.

4.9   Explain why it was necessary to declare `owl:Class` as a subclass of `rdfs:Class`.

4.10  In chapter 3 we presented an axiomatic semantics for RDF. A similar axiomatic semantics can be developed for OWL. Define the axiomatic semantics of `intersectionOf`.

4.11  Define the axiomatic semantics of `inverseOf`.

4.12  In this exercise you are asked to develop an axiomatic semantics for cardinality restrictions.

(a)  Define `noRepeatsList`. $L$ is a "no repeats list" if there is not an element that occurs in $L$ more than once. The concept is not part of the OWL language but will be used to count the elements for cardinality restrictions.

(b)  Define `minCardinality` and `maxCardinality` as properties with domain `Restriction` and range `NonNegativeInteger`.

(c)  Give an axiom that captures the meaning of `minCardinality`: If $onProperty(R, P)$ and $minCardinality(R, n)$ then $x$ is an instance of $R$ if, and only if, there is a "no repeats list" $L$ of length $\geq n$, such that $P(x, y)$ for all $y \in L$.

(d)  Express the meaning of `maxCardinality` in a similar way.

4.13  Have a look at some ontologies at
<http://www.daml.org/ontologies>.

4.14  Write your own ontologies in OWL.

4.15  OIL is a predecessor of OWL. Read the pages about the OIL language and some of the example ontologies. Compare the OIL language to the OWL language, paying attention both to commonalities and differences.

4.16  Compare the online documents on OWL to those for DAML+OIL.

4.17  Rewrite some examples from the DAML+OIL documents using OWL terminology.

4.18  Try to think of features that are still missing in OWL. *Hint:* Think of projects and persons involved. What should be true for each project, and what for each person (to be valuable to their company)? Can you express these conditions in OWL?

# 5 *Logic and Inference: Rules*

## 5.1 Introduction

From an abstract viewpoint, the subjects of the previous chapters were related to the *representation of knowledge*: knowledge about the content of Web resources, and knowledge about the concepts of a domain of discourse and their relationships (ontology).

Knowledge representation had been studied long before the emergence of the World Wide Web, in the area of artificial intelligence and, before that, in philosophy. In fact, it can be traced back to ancient Greece; Aristotle is considered to be the father of logic. Logic is still the foundation of knowledge representation, particularly in the form of *predicate logic* (also known as *first-order logic*). Here we list a few reasons for the popularity and importance of logic:

- It provides a high-level language in which knowledge can be expressed in a transparent way. And it has a high expressive power.

- It has a well-understood formal semantics, which assigns an unambiguous meaning to logical statements.

- There is precise notion of logical consequence, which determines whether a statement follows semantically from a set of other statements (premises). In fact, the primary original motivation of logic was the study of objective laws of logical consequence.

- There exist proof systems that can automatically derive statements syntactically from a set of premises.

- There exist proof systems for which semantic logical consequence coincides with syntactic derivation within the proof system. Proof systems should be sound (all derived statements follow semantically from the premises) and complete (all logical consequences of the premises can be derived in the proof system).

- Predicate logic is unique in the sense that sound and complete proof systems do exist. More expressive logics (higher-order logics) do not have such proof systems.

- Because of the existence of proof systems, it is possible to trace the proof that leads to a logical consequence. In this sense, the logic can provide explanations for answers.

The languages of RDF and OWL (Lite and DL) can be viewed as specializations of predicate logic. The correspondence was illustrated by the axiomatic semantics in the form of logical axioms.

One justification for the existence of such specialized languages is that they provide a syntax that fits well with the intended use (in our case, Web languages based on tags). The other major justification is that they define reasonable subsets of logic. As mentioned in section 4.1, there is a trade-off between the expressive power and the computational complexity of certain logics: the more expressive the language, the less efficient (in the worst case) the corresponding proof systems. As we stated, OWL Lite and OWL DL correspond roughly to a description logic, a subset of predicate logic for which efficient proof systems exist.

Another subset of predicate logic with efficient proof systems comprises the so-called *rule systems* (also known as *Horn logic* or *definite logic programs*) . A rule has the form

$$A_1, \ldots A_n \rightarrow B$$

where $A_i$ and $B$ are atomic formulas. In fact, there are two intuitive ways of reading such a rule:

1. If $A_1, \ldots, A_n$ are known to be true, then $B$ is also true. Rules with this interpretation are referred to as *deductive rules*.

2. If the conditions $A_1, \ldots, A_n$ are true, then carry out the action $B$. Rules with this interpretation are referred to as *reactive rules*.

Both views have important applications. However, in this chapter we take the deductive approach. We study the language and possible queries that one can ask, as well as appropriate answers. Also we outline the working of a proof mechanism that can return such answers.

It is interesting to note that description logics and Horn logic are orthogonal in the sense that neither of them is a subset of the other. For example, it is impossible to assert that persons who study and live in the same city are "home students" in OWL, whereas this can be done easily using rules:

$$studies(X, Y), lives(X, Z), loc(Y, U), loc(Z, U) \rightarrow homeStudent(X)$$

On the other hand, rules cannot assert the information that a person is either a man or a woman, whereas this information is easily expressed in OWL using disjoint union.

Then we turn our attention to another kind of rules. We give a simple example. Suppose an online vendor wants to give a special discount if it is a customer's birthday. An easy way to represent this application with rules is as follows:

$R1$ : If birthday, then special discount.

$R2$ : If not birthday, then not special discount.

This solution works properly in case the birthday is known. But imagine a customer who refuses to provide his birthday because of privacy concerns. In such a case, the preceding rules cannot be applied because their premises are not known. To capture this situation we need to write something like

$R1$ : If birthday, then special discount.

$R2'$ : If birthday is not known, then not special discount.

However, the premise of rule $R2'$ is not within the expressive power of predicate logic. Thus we need a new kind of rule system. We note that the solution with rules $R1$ and $R2$ works in case we have complete information about the situation (for example, either birthday or not birthday). The new kind of rule system will find application in cases where the available information is incomplete.

Predicate logic and its special cases are monotonic in the following sense: if a conclusion can be drawn, it remains valid even if new knowledge becomes available. But if rule $R2'$ is applied to derive "not special discount," then this conclusion may become invalid if the customer's birthday becomes known at a later stage and it happens to coincide with the purchase date. Thus we talk of *nonmonotonic rules* to distinguish them from monotonic rules (which are a special case of predicate logic). In this chapter, we will discuss both monotonic and nonmonotonic rules.

Our final concern will be the exchange of rules across different applications. For example, an online store might wish to make its pricing, refund, and privacy policies, which are expressed using rules, accessible to intelligent agents. The Semantic Web approach is to express the knowledge in a machine-accessible way using one of the Web languages we have already discussed. In this chapter, we show how rules can be expressed in XML-like languages ("rule markup languages"). Some applications of rule systems are discussed in chapter 6.

In this chapter we give an example using monotonic rules (a subset of predicate logic called Horn logic) in section 5.2. Sections 5.3 and 5.4 describe the syntax and semantics of Horn logic, and section 5.5 describes the syntax of nonmonotonic rules.

Section 5.6 presents an example of nonmonotonic rules. Finally, sections 5.7 and 5.8 describe an XML-based representation of monotonic and nonmonotonic rules.

## 5.2 Example of Monotonic Rules: Family Relationships

Imagine a database of facts about some family relationships. Suppose that the database contains facts about the following *base predicates*:

| | |
|---|---|
| $mother(X, Y)$ | $X$ is the mother of $Y$ |
| $father(X, Y)$ | $X$ is the father of $Y$ |
| $male(X)$ | $X$ is male |
| $female(X)$ | $X$ is female |

Then we can infer further relationships using appropriate rules. First, we can define a predicate *parent*: a parent is either a father or a mother.

$$mother(X, Y) \rightarrow parent(X, Y)$$
$$father(X, Y) \rightarrow parent(X, Y)$$

Then we can define a brother to be a male person sharing a parent:

$$male(X), parent(P, X), parent(P, Y), notSame(X, Y) \rightarrow$$
$$brother(X, Y)$$

The predicate *notSame* denotes inequality; we assume that such facts are kept in a database. Of course, every practical logical system offers convenient ways of expressing equality and inequality, but we chose the abstract solution to keep the discussion general.

Similarly, *sister* is defined as follows:

$$female(X), parent(P, X), parent(P, Y), notSame(X, Y) \rightarrow sister(X, Y)$$

An uncle is a brother of a parent:

$$brother(X, P), parent(P, Y) \rightarrow uncle(X, Y)$$

A grandmother is the mother of a parent:

$$mother(X, P), parent(P, Y) \rightarrow grandmother(X, Y)$$

An ancestor is either a parent or an ancestor of a parent:

$$parent(X, Y) \rightarrow ancestor(X, Y)$$

$$ancestor(X, P), parent(P, Y) \rightarrow ancestor(X, Y)$$

## 5.3 Monotonic Rules: Syntax

Let us consider a simple rule stating that all loyal customers aged over 60 are entitled to a special discount:

$$loyalCustomer(X), age(X) > 60 \rightarrow discount(X)$$

We distinguish some ingredients of rules:

- *variables*, which are placeholders for values: $X$

- *constants*, which denote fixed values: $60$

- *predicates*, which relate objects: $loyalCustomer, >$

- *function symbols*, which return a value for certain arguments: $age$

### 5.3.1   Rules

A rule has the form

$$B_1, \ldots, B_n \to A$$

where $A, B_1, \ldots, B_n$ are atomic formulas. $A$ is the *head* of the rule, and $B_1, \ldots, B_n$ are the *premises* of the rule. The set $\{B_1, \ldots, B_n\}$ is referred to as the *body* of the rule.

The commas in the rule body are read conjunctively: if $B_1$ and $B_2$ and ... and $B_n$ are true, then $A$ is also true (or equivalently, to prove $A$ it is sufficient to prove all $B_1, \ldots, B_n$).

Note that variables may occur in $A, B_1, \ldots, B_n$. For example,

$$loyalCustomer(X), age(X) > 60 \to discount(X)$$

This rule is applied for *any* customer: if a customer happens to be loyal and over 60, then she gets the discount. In other words, the variable $X$ is implicitly universally quantified (using $\forall X$). In general, all variables occurring in a rule are implicitly universally quantified.

In summary, a rule $r$

$$B_1, \ldots, B_n \to A$$

is interpreted as the following formula, denoted by $pl(r)$:

$$\forall X_1 \ldots \forall X_k((B_1 \wedge \ldots \wedge B_n) \to A)$$

or equivalently,

$$\forall X_1 \ldots \forall X_k(A \vee \neg B_1 \vee \ldots \vee \neg B_n)$$

where $X_1, \ldots, X_k$ are all variables occurring in $A, B_1, \ldots, B_n$.

### 5.3.2   Facts

A fact is an atomic formula, such as $loyalCustomer(a345678)$; it says that the customer with ID a345678 is loyal. The variables of a fact are implicitly universally quantified.

### 5.3.3   Logic Programs

A logic program $P$ is a finite set of facts and rules. Its predicate logic translation $pl(P)$ is the set of all predicate logic interpretations of rules and facts in $P$.

### 5.3.4 Goals

A goal denotes a query $G$ asked to a logic program. It has the form

$$B_1, \ldots, B_n \rightarrow$$

If $n = 0$ we have the *empty goal* $\square$.

Our next task is to interpret goals in predicate logic. Using the ideas we developed before (interpretations of commas as conjunction, implicit universal quantification) we get the following interpretation:

$$\forall X_1 \ldots \forall X_k(\neg B_1 \vee \ldots \vee \neg B_n)$$

This formula is the same as $pl(r)$, with the only difference that the rule head $A$ is omitted[1].

An equivalent representation in predicate logic is

$$\neg \exists X_1 \ldots \exists X_k(B_1 \wedge \ldots \wedge B_n)$$

where $X_1, \ldots, X_k$ are all variables occurring in $B_1, \ldots, B_n$. Let us briefly explain this formula. Suppose we know

$$p(a)$$

and we have the goal

$$p(X) \rightarrow$$

Actually, we want to know whether there is a value for which $p$ is true. We expect a positive answer because of the fact $p(a)$. Thus $p(X)$ is existentially quantified. But then why do we negate the formula? The explanation is that we use a proof technique from mathematics called *proof by contradiction*. This technique proves that a statement $A$ follows from a statement $B$ by assuming that $A$ is false and deriving a contradiction, when combined with $B$. Then $A$ *must* follow from $B$.

In logic programming we prove that a goal can be answered positively by negating the goal and proving that we get a contradiction using the logic program. For example, given the logic program

$$p(a)$$

---

1. Note that the formula is equivalent to $\forall X_1 \ldots \forall X_k(false \vee \neg B_1 \vee \ldots \vee \neg B_n)$, so a missing rule head can be thought of as a contradiction $false$.

and the goal

$$\neg \exists X p(X)$$

we get a logical contradiction: the second formula says that no element has the property $p$, but the first formula says that the value of $a$ does have the property $p$. Thus $\exists X p(X)$ follows from $p(a)$.

## 5.4   Monotonic Rules: Semantics

### 5.4.1   Predicate Logic Semantics

One way of answering a query is to use the predicate logic interpretation of rules, facts, and queries, and to make use of the well-known semantics of predicate logic. To be more precise, given a logic program $P$ and a query

$$B_1, \ldots, B_n \rightarrow$$

with the variables $X_1, \ldots, X_k$, we answer positively if, and only if,

$$pl(P) \models \exists X_1 \ldots \exists X_k (B_1 \wedge \ldots \wedge B_n) \tag{1}$$

or equivalently, if

$$pl(P) \cup \{\neg \exists X_1 \ldots \exists X_k (B_1 \wedge \ldots \wedge B_n)\} \text{ is unsatisfiable} \tag{2}$$

In other words, we give a positive answer if the predicate logic representation of the program $P$, together with the predicate logic interpretation of the query, is unsatisfiable (a contradiction).

The formal definition of the semantic concepts of predicate logic is found in the literature. Here we just give an informal presentation. The components of the logical language (signature) may have any meaning we like. A predicate logic *model* $\mathcal{A}$ assigns a certain meaning. In particular, it consists of

- a *domain dom($\mathcal{A}$)*, a nonempty set of objects about which the formulas make statements

- an element from the domain for each constant

- a concrete function on $dom(\mathcal{A})$ for every function symbol

- a concrete relation on $dom(\mathcal{A})$ for every predicate

The meanings of the logical connectives $\neg, \vee, \wedge, \rightarrow, \forall, \exists$ are defined according to their intuitive meaning: not, or, and, implies, for all, there is. This way we define when a formula is true in a model $\mathcal{A}$, denoted as $\mathcal{A} \models \varphi$.

A formula $\varphi$ *follows* from a set $M$ of formulas if $\varphi$ is true in all models $\mathcal{A}$ in which $M$ is true (that is, all formulas in $M$ are true in $\mathcal{A}$).

Now we are able to explain (1) and (2). Regardless of how we interpret the constants, predicates, and function symbols occurring in $P$ and the query, once the predicate logic interpretation of $P$ is true, $\exists X_1 \ldots \exists X_k (B_1 \wedge \ldots \wedge B_n)$ must be true, too. That is, there are values for the variables $X_1, \ldots, X_k$ such that all atomic formulas $B_i$ become true.

For example, suppose $P$ is the program

$$p(a)$$

$$p(X) \rightarrow q(X)$$

Consider the query

$$q(X) \rightarrow$$

Clearly, $q(a)$ follows from $pl(P)$. Therefore, $\exists X q(X)$ follows from $pl(P)$, thus $pl(P) \cup \{\neg \exists X q(X)\}$ is unsatisfiable, and we give a positive answer. But if we consider the query

$$q(b) \rightarrow$$

then we must give a negative answer because $q(b)$ does not follow from $pl(P)$.

The other kind of semantics for logic programs, least Herbrand model semantics, requires more technical treatment, and is not discussed here.

## 5.4.2 Ground and Parameterized Witnesses

So far we have focused on yes/no answers to queries. However, such answers are not necessarily optimal. Suppose that we have the fact

$$p(a)$$

and the query

$$p(X) \rightarrow$$

The answer yes is correct but not satisfactory. It resembles the joke where you are asked, "Do you know what time it is?", and you look at your watch and answer "yes." In our example, the appropriate answer is a substitution

$$\{X/a\}$$

which gives an instantiation for $X$, making the answer positive. The constant $a$ is called a *ground witness*. Given the facts

$$p(a)$$
$$p(b)$$

there are two ground witnesses to the same query: $a$ and $b$. Or equivalently, we should return the substitutions:

$$\{X/a\}$$
$$\{X/b\}$$

While valuable, ground witnesses are not always the optimal answer. Consider the logic program

$$add(X, 0, X)$$
$$add(X, Y, Z) \rightarrow add(X, s(Y), s(Z))$$

This program computes addition, if we read $s$ as the "successor function," which returns as value the value of its argument plus 1. The third argument of $add$ computes the sum of its first two arguments. Consider the query

$$add(X, s^8(0), Z) \rightarrow$$

Possible ground witnesses are determined by the substitutions

$$\{X/0, Z/s^8(0)\}$$
$$\{X/s(0), Z/s^9(0)\}$$
$$\{X/s(s(0)), Z/s^{10}(0)\}$$
$$\ldots$$

However, the *parameterized witness* $Z = s^8(X)$ is the most general way to witness the existential query

$$\exists X \exists Z \; add(X, s^8(0), Z)$$

The computation of such most general witnesses is the primary aim of the proof theory, called SLD resolution,[2] the presentation of which is beyond the scope of this book.

## 5.5   Nonmonotonic Rules: Motivation and Syntax

### 5.5.1   Informal Discussion

Now we turn our attention to nonmonotonic rule systems. So far, once the premises of a rule were proved, the rule could be applied and its head could be derived as a conclusion. In nonmonotonic rule systems, a rule may not be applied even if all premises are known because we have to consider contrary reasoning chains. In general, the rules we consider from now on are called *defeasible*, because they can be defeated by other rules. To allow conflicts between rules, *negated atomic formulas* may occur in the head and the body of rules. For example, we may write

$$p(X) \rightarrow q(X)$$
$$r(X) \rightarrow \neg q(X)$$

To distinguish between defeasible rules and standard, monotonic rules, we use a different arrow:

$$p(X) \Rightarrow q(X)$$
$$r(X) \Rightarrow \neg q(X)$$

In this example, given also the facts

$$p(a)$$
$$r(a)$$

we conclude neither $q(a)$ nor $\neg q(a)$. It is a typical example of two rules blocking each other. This conflict may be resolved using *priorities among rules*. Suppose we knew somehow that the first rule is stronger than the second; then we could indeed derive $q(a)$.

Priorities arise naturally in practice, and may be based on various principles:

---

2. SLD resolution stands for "selective linear resolution for definite clauses."

- The source of one rule may be more reliable than the source of the second rule, or may have higher authority. For example, in law, federal law pre-empts state law. And in business administration, higher management has more authority than middle management.

- One rule may be preferred over another because it is more recent.

- One rule may be preferred over another because it is more specific. A typical example is a general rule with some exceptions; in such cases, the exceptions are stronger than the general rule.

Specificity may often be computed based on the given rules, but the other two principles cannot be determined from the logical formalization. There-fore, we abstract from the specific prioritization principle used, and assume the existence of an *external priority relation* on the set of rules. To express the relation syntactically, we extend the rule syntax to include a unique label, for example,

$$r_1 : p(X) \Rightarrow q(X)$$
$$r_2 : r(X) \Rightarrow \neg q(X)$$

Then we can write

$$r_1 > r_2$$

to specify that $r_1$ is stronger than $r_2$.

We do not impose many conditions on $>$. It is not even required that the rules form a complete ordering. We only require the priority relation to be acyclic. That is, it is impossible to have cycles of the form

$$r_1 > r_2 > \ldots > r_n > r_1$$

Note that priorities are meant to resolve conflicts among *competing rules*. In simple cases two rules are competing only if the head of one rule is the nega-tion of the head of the other. But in applications it is often the case that once a predicate $p$ is derived, some other predicates are excluded from holding. For example, an investment consultant may base his recommendations on three levels of risk investors are willing to take: low, moderate, and high. Obvi-ously, only one risk level per investor is allowed to hold at any given time. Technically, these situations are modeled by maintaining a conflict set $C(L)$ for each literal $L$. $C(L)$ always contains the negation of $L$ but may contain more literals.

### 5.5.2 Definition of the Syntax

A *defeasible rule* has the form

$$r : L_1, \ldots, L_n \Rightarrow L$$

where $r$ is the *label*, $\{L_1, \ldots, L_n\}$ the *body* (or *premises*), and $L$ the *head* of the rule. $L, L_1, \ldots, L_n$ are positive or negative literals (a literal is an atomic formula $p(t_1, \ldots, t_m)$ or its negation $\neg p(t_1, \ldots, t_m)$). No function symbols may occur in the rule.[3] Sometimes we denote the head of a rule as $head(r)$, and its body as $body(r)$. Slightly abusing notation, sometimes we use the label $r$ to refer to the whole rule.

A *defeasible logic program* is a triple $(F, R, >)$ consisting of a set $F$ of facts, a finite set $R$ of defeasible rules, and an acyclic binary relation $>$ on $R$ (precisely, a set of pairs $r > r'$ where $r$ and $r'$ are labels of rules in $R$).

## 5.6 Example of Nonmonotonic Rules: Brokered Trade

This example shows how rules can be used in an electronic commerce application (which will ideally run on the Semantic Web). Brokered trades take place via an independent third party, the broker. The broker matches the buyer's requirements and the sellers' capabilities, and proposes a transaction when both parties can be satisfied by the trade.

As a concrete application we will discuss apartment renting,[4] an activity that is common and often tedious and time-consuming. Appropriate Web services can reduce the effort considerably. We begin by presenting the potential renter's requirements.

Carlos is looking for an apartment of at least 45 sq m with at least two bedrooms. If it is on the third floor or higher, the house must have an elevator. Also, pet animals must be allowed.

Carlos is willing to pay $300 for a centrally located 45 sq m apartment, and $250 for a similar flat in the suburbs. In addition, he is willing to pay an extra $5 per square meter for a larger apartment, and $2 per square meter for a garden.

---

3. This restriction is imposed for technical reasons, the discussion of which is beyond the scope of this chapter.
4. In this case, the landlord takes the role of the abstract seller.

He is unable to pay more than \$400 in total. If given the choice, he would go for the cheapest option. His second priority is the presence of a garden; his lowest priority is additional space.

### 5.6.1   Formalization of Carlos's Requirements

We use the following predicates to describe properties of apartments:

| | |
|---|---:|
| $size(x, y)$ | $y$ is the size of apartment $x$ (in sq m) |
| $bedrooms(x, y)$ | $x$ has $y$ bedrooms |
| $price(x, y)$ | $y$ is the price for $x$ |
| $floor(x, y)$ | $x$ is on the $y$th floor |
| $garden(x, y)$ | $x$ has a garden of size $y$ |
| $lift(x)$ | there is an elevator in the house of $x$ |
| $pets(x)$ | pets are allowed in $x$ |
| $central(x)$ | $x$ is centrally located |

We also make use of the following predicates:

| | |
|---|---:|
| $acceptable(x)$ | flat $x$ satisfies Carlos's requirements |
| $offer(x, y)$ | Carlos is willing to pay \$ $y$ for flat $x$ |

Now we present Carlos's firm requirements. Any apartment is a priori acceptable.

$$r_1 : \Rightarrow acceptable(X)$$

However, $Y$ is unacceptable if one of Carlos's requirements is not met.

$$r_2 : \ bedrooms(X, Y), Y < 2 \Rightarrow \neg acceptable(X)$$
$$r_3 : \ size(X, Y), Y < 45 \Rightarrow \neg acceptable(X)$$
$$r_4 : \ \neg pets(X) \Rightarrow \neg acceptable(X)$$
$$r_5 : \ floor(X, Y), Y > 2, \neg lift(X) \Rightarrow \neg acceptable(X)$$
$$r_6 : \ price(X, Y), Y > 400 \Rightarrow \neg acceptable(X)$$

Rules $r_2$-$r_6$ are exceptions to rule $r_1$, so we add

$$r_2 > r_1, \ r_3 > r_1, \ r_4 > r_1, \ r_5 > r_1, \ r_6 > r_1$$

Next we calculate the price Carlos is willing to pay for an apartment.

$r_7 : size(X, Y), Y \geq 45, garden(X, Z), central(X) \Rightarrow offer(X, 300 + 2Z + 5(Y - 45))$

$r_8 : size(X, Y), Y \geq 45, garden(X, Z), \neg central(X) \Rightarrow offer(X, 250 + 2Z + 5(Y - 45))$

An apartment is only acceptable if the amount Carlos is willing to pay is not less than the price specified by the landlord (we assume no bargaining can take place).

$r_9 : offer(X, Y), price(X, Z), Y < Z \Rightarrow \neg acceptable(X)$

$r_9 > r_1$

## 5.6.2   Representation of Available Apartments

Each available apartment is given a unique name, and its properties are represented as facts. For example, apartment $a_1$ might be described as follows:

$bedrooms(a_1, 1)$

$size(a_1, 50)$

$central(a_1)$

$floor(a_1, 1)$

$\neg lift(a_1)$

$pets(a_1)$

$garden(a_1, 0)$

$price(a_1, 300)$

The description of the available apartments are summarized in table 5.1. In practice, the flats on offer could be stored in a relational database.

If we match Carlos's requirements and the available apartments, we see that

- flat $a_1$ is not acceptable because it has one bedroom only (rule $r_2$)

- flats $a_4$ and $a_6$ are unacceptable because pets are not allowed (rule $r_4$)

- for $a_2$, Carlos is willing to pay $300, but the price is higher (rules $r_7$ and $r_9$)

- flats $a_3, a_5,$ and $a_7$ are acceptable (rule $r_1$)

| Flat | Bedrooms | Size | Central | Floor | Lift | Pets | Garden | Price |
|------|----------|------|---------|-------|------|------|--------|-------|
| $a_1$ | 1 | 50 | yes | 1 | no | yes | 0 | 300 |
| $a_2$ | 2 | 45 | yes | 0 | no | yes | 0 | 335 |
| $a_3$ | 2 | 65 | no | 2 | no | yes | 0 | 350 |
| $a_4$ | 2 | 55 | no | 1 | yes | no | 15 | 330 |
| $a_5$ | 3 | 55 | yes | 0 | no | yes | 15 | 350 |
| $a_6$ | 2 | 60 | yes | 3 | no | no | 0 | 370 |
| $a_7$ | 3 | 65 | yes | 1 | no | yes | 12 | 375 |

**Table 5.1**   Available apartments

### 5.6.3   Selecting an Apartment

So far we have identified the apartments acceptable to Carlos. This selection is valuable in itself, since it reduces the focus to relevant flats, which may then be physically inspected. But it is also possible to reduce the number further, even down to a single apartment, by taking further preferences into account. Carlos's preferences are based on price, garden size, and size, in that order. We represent them as follows:

$$r_{10} :\ cheapest(X) \Rightarrow rent(X)$$

$$r_{11} :\ cheapest(X), largestGarden(X) \Rightarrow rent(X)$$

$$r_{12} :\ cheapest(X), largestGarden(X), largest(X) \Rightarrow rent(X)$$

$$r_{12} > r_{10}$$

$$r_{12} > r_{11}$$

$$r_{11} > r_{10}$$

Also, we need to specify that at most one apartment can be rented, using conflict sets:

$$C(rent(x)) = \{\neg rent(x)\} \cup \{rent(y) \mid y \neq x\}$$

The prerequisites of these rules can be derived from the set of acceptable apartments using further rules. Here we keep the discussion simple by just stating the facts for our example:

$$cheapest(a_3)$$

$$cheapest(a_5)$$

$$largest(a_3)$$

$$largest(a_7)$$

$$largestGarden(a_5)$$

Now the theory is able to derive the decision to rent $a_5$:

- Rule $r_{11}$ can be applied to $a_5$.

- Rule $r_{10}$ can be applied to $a_3$, thus establishing an attack. However, this attack is successfully countered because $r_{11}$ is stronger than $r_{10}$.

- This is indeed the only attack, because neither $r_{11}$ nor $r_{12}$ applies to any other apartment.

Thus a selection has been made, and Carlos will soon move in.

## 5.7 Rule Markup in XML: Monotonic Rules

Our aim here is to make knowledge in the form of rules machine-accessible, in accordance with the Semantic Web vision. We outline an encoding of monotonic rules in XML.

### 5.7.1 Terms

Terms are represented using XML tags <term>, <function>, <var>, and <const>. For example, the term

$$f(X, a, g(b, Y))$$

is represented as follows:

```
<term>
    <function>f</function>
    <term>
        <var>X</var>
    </term>
    <term>
        <const>a</const>
```

```
        </term>
        <term>
            <function>g</function>
            <term>
                <const>b</const>
            </term>
            <term>
                <var>Y</var>
            </term>
        </term>
    </term>
```

### 5.7.2   Atomic Formulas

For atomic formulas we use additionally the tag <atom> and the tag
<predicate>. For example, the formula

$$p(X, a, f(b, Y))$$

is represented as follows:

```
<atom>
    <predicate>p</predicate>
    <term>
        <var>X</var>
    </term>
    <term>
        <const>a</const>
    </term>
    <term>
        <function>f</function>
        <term>
            <const>b</const>
        </term>
        <term>
            <var>Y</var>
        </term>
    </term>
</atom>
```

Note that the distinction between function symbols, predicates, and constants, implicit in the logical syntax we have used so far, becomes explicit in XML.

### 5.7.3 Facts

A fact is just an atomic formula, enclosed by opening and closing <fact> tags. For example, the fact $p(a)$ is represented as follows:

```
<fact>
    <atom>
        <predicate>p</predicate>
        <term>
            <const>a</const>
        </term>
    </atom>
</fact>
```

### 5.7.4 Rules

A rule consist of a head and a body. A head is an atomic formula. The body is a (possibly empty) sequence of atomic formulas. We use new tags <rule>, <head>, and <body>. For example, the rule

$$p(X, a), q(Y, b) \rightarrow r(X, Y)$$

is represented as follows:

```
<rule>
    <head>
        <atom>
            <predicate>r</predicate>
            <term>
                <var>X</var>
            </term>
            <term>
                <var>Y</var>
            </term>
        </atom>
    </head>
```

```
<body>
   <atom>
      <predicate>p</predicate>
      <term>
         <var>X</var>
      </term>
      <term>
         <const>a</const>
      </term>
   </atom>
   <atom>
      <predicate>q</predicate>
      <term>
         <var>Y</var>
      </term>
      <term>
         <const>b</const>
      </term>
   </atom>
</body>
</rule>
```

### 5.7.5   Queries

Queries are represented as the bodies of rules, surrounded by <query> tags.

### 5.7.6   A DTD

A program consists of a number of rules and facts.

```
<!ELEMENT program ((rule|fact)*)>
```

A fact consists of an atomic formula.

```
<!ELEMENT fact (atom)>
```

A rule consists of a head and a body.

```
<!ELEMENT rule (head,body)>
```

A head consists of an atomic formula.

```
<!ELEMENT head (atom)>
```

A body is a list of atomic formulas.

```
<!ELEMENT body (atom*)>
```

An atomic formula consists of a predicate, followed by a number of terms.

```
<!ELEMENT atom (predicate,term*)>
```

A term is a constant, a variable, or a composite term consisting of a function symbol, followed by a number of terms.

```
<!ELEMENT term (const|var|(function,term*))>
```

Predicates, function symbols, constants, and variables are atomic types.

```
<!ELEMENT predicate (#PCDATA)>
<!ELEMENT function (#PCDATA)>
<!ELEMENT var (#PCDATA)>
<!ELEMENT const (#PCDATA)>
```

A query is a list of atomic formulas.

```
<!ELEMENT query (atom*)>
```

## 5.7.7   The Alternative Data Model of RuleML

RuleML is an important standardization effort in the area of rules in the context of the Semantic Web. It uses similar ideas to those presented in the DTD (figure 5.1 shows a comparison of tags used in the DTD and in RuleML.) But RuleML has developed an alternative data model that combines features of XML and RDF. Recall that in XML the order of elements is important, whereas it is ignored in RDF.

RuleML is at present based on XML but uses RDF-like "role tags," the position of which in an expression is irrelevant. For example, if we use the role tags <_head> and <_body>, the expression:

| Our DTD | RuleML |
|---------|---------|
| program | rulebase |
| fact | fact |
| rule | imp |
| head | _head |
| body | _body |
| atom | atom |
| atom* | and |
| predicate | rel |
| const | ind |
| var | var |

**Figure 5.1**   Monotonic rules DTD versus RuleML

```
<rule>
    <_head>
        <atom>
            <predicate>p</predicate>
            <term>
                <const>a</const>
            </term>
        </atom>
    </_head>
    <_body>
        <atom>
            <predicate>q</predicate>
            <term>
                <const>b</const>
            </term>
        </atom>
    </_body>
</rule>
```

is equivalent to

```
<rule>
    <_body>
        <atom>
```

```
            <predicate>q</predicate>
            <term>
                <const>b</const>
            </term>
        </atom>
    </_body>
    <_head>
        <atom>
            <predicate>p</predicate>
            <term>
                <const>a</const>
            </term>
        </atom>
    </_head>
</rule>
```

although they are different under the XML data model, in which the order is important. For a discussion of this idea, see Suggested Reading.

It should be clear that we can express in XML not only programs and queries but also substitutions and proofs.

## 5.8   Rule Markup in XML: Nonmonotonic Rules

Compared to monotonic rules, nonmonotonic rules have the following syntactic differences:

- There are no function symbols; therefore the term structure is flat.

- Negated atoms may occur in the head and the body of a rule.

- Each rule has a label.

- Apart from rules and facts, a program also contains priority statements.

### 5.8.1   An Example

Consider the defeasible program

$$r_1 : \; p(X) \Rightarrow s(X)$$
$$r_2 : \; q(X) \Rightarrow \neg s(X)$$

$$p(a)$$

$$q(a)$$

$$r_1 > r_2$$

We use a `<stronger>` tag to represent priorities, and an ID label in rules to denote their name.

Rule $r_1$ is represented as follows:

```
<rule id="r1">
    <head>
        <atom>
            <predicate>s</predicate>
            <term>
                <var>X</var>
            </term>
        </atom>
    </head>
    <body>
        <atom>
            <predicate>p</predicate>
            <term>
                <var>X</var>
            </term>
        </atom>
    </body>
</rule>
```

Rule $r_2$ is represented accordingly. The fact $p(a)$ is represented as follows:

```
<fact>
    <atom>
        <predicate>p</predicate>
        <term>
            <const>a</const>
        </term>
    </atom>
</fact>
```

And the priority relation $r_1 > r_2$ is represented as follows:

```
<stronger superior="r1" inferior="r2"/>
```

## 5.8.2  A DTD

A program consists of a number of rules, facts, and priority relations.

```
<!ELEMENT program ((rule|fact|stronger)*)>
```

A fact consists of an atomic formula or its negation.

```
<!ELEMENT fact (atom|neg)>
<!ELEMENT neg (atom)>
```

A rule consists of a head and a body element, and an `id` attribute.

```
<!ELEMENT rule (head,body)>
<!ATTLIST rule
    id ID #IMPLIED>
```

The rule head and body are defined as for monotonic rules, but may contain negated atoms.

```
<!ELEMENT head (atom|neg)>
<!ELEMENT body ((atom|neg)*)>
```

An atomic formula consists of a predicate, followed by a number of variables and constants.

```
<!ELEMENT atom (predicate,(var|const)*)>
```

A priority element uses two attributes, referring to the superior and the inferior rule.

```
<!ELEMENT stronger EMPTY)>
<!ATTLIST stronger
    superior  IDREF  #REQUIRED>
    inferior  IDREF  #REQUIRED>
```

Predicates, constants, and variables are atomic types.

```
<!ELEMENT predicate (#PCDATA)>
<!ELEMENT var (#PCDATA)>
<!ELEMENT const (#PCDATA)>
```

A query is a list of atomic formulas.

```
<!ELEMENT query (atom*)>
```

## 5.9   Summary

- Horn logic is a subset of predicate logic that allows efficient reasoning. It forms a subset orthogonal to description logics.

- Horn logic is the basis of monotonic rules.

- Nonmonotonic rules are useful in situations where the available information is incomplete. They are rules that may be overridden by contrary evidence (other rules).

- Priorities are used to resolve some conflicts between nonmonotonic rules.

- The representation of rules in XML-like languages is straightforward.

## Suggested Reading

Monotonic rules are a standard topic in logic. More information can be found in relevant textbooks, such as the following:

- E. Burke and E. Foxley. *Logic and Its Applications*. Upper Saddle River, N.J: Prentice Hall, 1996.

- M. A. Covington, D. Nute, and A. Vellino. *Prolog Programming in Depth*, 2nd ed. Upper Saddle River, N.J: Prentice Hall, 1997.

- A. Nerode and R. A. Shore. *Logic for Applications*. New York: Springer, 1997.

- U. Nilsson and J. Maluszynski. *Logic, Programming and Prolog*, 2nd ed. New York: Wiley, 1995.

- N. Nissanke. *Introductory Logic and Sets for Computer Scientists*. Boston: Addison-Wesley, 1998.

Nonmonotonic rules are a quite new topic. Information can be found in Covington, Nute and Vellino, *Prolog Programming in Depth*, and in the following:

- G. Antoniou, D. Billington, G. Governatori, and M. J. Maher. Representation results for defeasible logic. *ACM Transactions on Computational Logic* 2 (April 2001): 255-287.

- B. N. Grosof. Prioritized Conflict Handling for Logic Programs. In *Proceedings of the International Logic Programming Symposium*. 1997, 197-211.

- B. N. Grosof, Y. Labrou, and H. Y. Chan. A Declarative Approach to Business Rules in Contracts: Courteous Logic Programs in XML. In *Proceedings of the 1st ACM Conference on Electronic Commerce (EC-99)*, 1999.

- D. Nute. Defeasible Logic. In *Handbook of Logic in Artificial Intelligence and Logic Programming Vol. 3*, D. M. Gabbay, C. J. Hogger, and J. A. Robinson, eds. New York: Oxford University Press, 1994.

- <http://www.informatik.uni- bremen.de/~ga/research/ruleml.html>.

General information about markup languages for rules and their use in the Semantic Web can be found at the RuleML Web site:

- <http://www.dfki.uni-kl.de/ruleml/>.

A paper describing the RuleML data model in some detail is

- H. Boley. The Rule Markup Language: RDF-XML Data Model, XML Schema Hierarchy, and XSL Transformations. 2001.
  <http://www.dfki.uni-kl.de/~boley/ruleml-mht.pdf>.

TRIPLE is an inference system designed for the Semantic Web. Details can be found at

- <http://triple.semanticweb.org/>.

## Exercises and Projects

5.1 We refer to the example in section 5.2. Define the predicates aunt, grandfather, sibling, and descendant.

5.2 Consider a graph with nodes and directed edges, and let an edge from node $a$ to node $b$ be represented by a fact $edge(a, b)$. Define a binary predicate *path* that is true for nodes $c$ and $d$ if, and only if, there is a path from $c$ to $d$ in the graph.

5.3 Propose a combination of nonmonotonic rules with ontologies. In particular, propose an integration such that

  (a) an ontology is used to derive some facts,

  (b) defeasible rules may use facts from (a),

(c) the predicates of rule heads do not occur in the ontology (that is, rules may only use, but not derive, new ontological knowledge).

5.4   For monotonic rules, propose a proof markup in XML. Among others, you should define markup for substitutions and SLD derivations (for those familiar with SLD resolution).

5.5   Determine which constructs of RDFS and OWL can be expressed using monotonic rules. For example, the subclass relation is represented as $c(X) \rightarrow c'(X)$ ($c$ is a subclass of $c'$).

# 6 *Applications*

## 6.1 Introduction

In this chapter we describe a number of applications in which the technology described in this book have been or could be put to use. We have, aimed to describe realistic scenarios only; if the scenarios are not already implemented, they are at least being seriously considered by major industrial firms in different sectors.

The descriptions in this chapter give a general overview of the kinds of uses to which Semantic Web technology can be applied. These include horizontal information products, data integration, skill-finding, a think tank portal, e-learning, web services, multimedia collection indexing, on-line procurement, and device interoperability.

## 6.2 Horizontal Information Products at Elsevier

### 6.2.1 The Setting

Elsevier is a leading scientific publisher. Its products, like those of many of its competitors, are organized mainly along traditional lines: subscriptions to journals. Online availability of these journals has until now not really changed the organization of the productline. Although individual papers are available online, this is only in the form in which they appeared in the journal, and collections of articles are organized according to the journal in which they appeared. Customers of Elsevier can take subscriptions to online content, but again these subscriptions are organized according to the traditional product lines: journals or bundles of journals.

## 6.2.2   The Problem

These traditional journals can be described as vertical products: the products are split up into a number of separate columns (e.g., biology, chemistry, medicine), and each product covers one such column (or more likely part of one such column). However, with the rapid developments in the various sciences (information sciences, life sciences, physical sciences), the traditional division into separate sciences covered by distinct journals is no longer satisfactory. Customers of Elsevier are instead interested in covering certain topic areas that spread across the traditional disciplines. A pharmaceutical company wants to buy from Elsevier all the information it has about, say, Alzheimer's disease, regardless of whether this comes from a biology journal, a medical journal, or a chemistry journal. Thus, the demand is rather for horizontal products: all the information Elsevier has about a given topic, sliced across all the separate traditional disciplines and journal boundaries.

Currently, it is difficult for large publishers like Elsevier to offer such horizontal products. The information published by Elsevier is locked inside the separate journals, each with its own indexing system, organized according to different physical, syntactic, and semantic standards. Barriers of physical and syntactic heterogeneity can be solved. Elsevier has translated much of its content to an XML format that allows cross-journal querying. However, the semantic problem remains largely unsolved. Of course, it is possible to search across multiple journals for articles containing the same keywords, but given the extensive homonym and synonym problems within and between the various disciplines, this is unlikely to provide satisfactory results. What is needed is a way to search the various journals on a coherent set of concepts against which all of these journals are indexed.

## 6.2.3   The Contribution of Semantic Web Technology

Ontologies and thesauri, which can be seen as very lightweight ontologies, have proved to be a key technology for effective information access because they help to overcome some of the problems of free-text search by relating and grouping relevant terms in a specific domain as well as providing a controlled vocabulary for indexing information. A number of thesauri have been developed in different domains of expertise. Examples from the area of medical information include MeSH[1] and Elsevier's life science thesaurus

---

1. <http://www.nlm.nih.gov/mesh>.

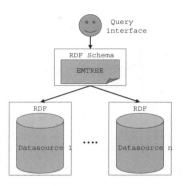

**Figure 6.1**   Querying across data sources at Elsevier

EMTREE.[2] These thesauri are already used to access information sources like MBASE[3] or Science Direct®, however, currently there are no links between the different information sources and the specific thesauri used to index and query these sources.

Elsevier is experimenting with the possibility of providing access to multiple information sources in the area of the life sciences through a single interface, using EMTREE as the single underlying ontology against which all the vertical information sources are indexed (see figure 6.1).

Semantic Web technology plays multiple roles in this architecture. First, RDF is used as an interoperability format between heterogeneous data sources. Second, an ontology (in this case, EMTREE) is itself represented in RDF (even though this is by no means its native format). Each of the separate data sources is mapped onto this unifying ontology, which is then used as the single point of entry for all of these data sources.

This problem is not unique to Elsevier. The entire scientific publishing industry is currently struggling with these problems. Actually, Elsevier is one of the leaders in trying to adapt its contents to new styles of delivery and organization.

---

2. 42,000 indexing terms, 175,000 synonyms.
3. <http://www.embase.com>; 4000 journals, 8 million records.

## 6.3   Data Integration at Audi

### 6.3.1   The Setting

The problem described in the previous section is essentially a data integration problem. Elsevier is trying to solve this data integration problem for the benefit of its customers. But data integration is also a huge problem internal to companies. In fact, it is widely seen as the highest cost factor in the information technology budget of large companies. A company the size of Audi (51,000 employees, $22 billion revenue, 700,000 cars produced annually) operates thousands of databases, often duplicating and reduplicating the same information, and missing out on opportunities because data sources are not interconnected. Current practice is that corporations rely on costly manual code generation and point-to-point translation scripts for data integration.

### 6.3.2   The Problem

While traditional middleware improves and simplifies the integration process, it does not address the fundamental challenge of integration: the sharing of information based on the intended meaning, the semantics of the data.

### 6.3.3   The Contribution of Semantic Web Technology

Using ontologies as semantic data models can rationalize disparate data sources into one body of information. By creating ontologies for data and content sources and adding generic domain information, integration of disparate sources in the enterprise can be performed without disturbing existing applications. The ontology is mapped to the data sources (fields, records, files, documents), giving applications direct access to the data through the ontology.

We illustrate the general idea using a camera example.[4] Here is one way in which a particular data source or application may talk about cameras:

```
<SLR rdf:ID="Olympus-OM-10">
    <viewFinder>twin mirror</viewFinder>
    <optics>
      <Lens>
          <focal-length>75-300mm zoom</focal-length>
          <f-stop>4.0-4.5</f-stop>
```

---

4. By R. Costello, at <http://www.xfront.com/avoiding-syntactic-rigor-mortis.html>.

```
        </Lens>
      </optics>
      <shutter-speed>1/2000 sec. to 10 sec.</shutter-speed>
  </SLR>
```

This can be interpreted (by human readers) to say that Olympus-OM-10 is an SLR (which we know by previous experience to be a type of camera), that it has a twin-mirror viewfinder, and to give values for focal length range, f-stop intervals, and minimal and maximal shutter speed. Note that this interpretation is strictly done by a human reader. There is no way that a computer can know that Olympus-OM-10 is a type of SLR, whereas 75-300 mm is the value of the focal length.

This is just one way of syntactically encoding this information. A second data source may well have chosen an entirely different format:

```
<Camera rdf:ID="Olympus-OM-10">
    <viewFinder>twin mirror</viewFinder>
    <optics>
       <Lens>
           <size>300mm zoom</size>
           <aperture>4.5</aperture>
       </Lens>
    </optics>
    <shutter-speed>1/2000 sec. to 10 sec.</shutter-speed>
</Camera>
```

Human readers can see that these two different formats talk about the same object. After all, we know that SLR is a kind of camera, and that f-stop is a synonym for aperture. Of course, we can provide a simple ad hoc integration of these data sources by simply writing a translator from one to the other. But this would only solve this specific integration problem, and we would have to do the same again when we encountered the next data format for cameras.

Instead, we might well write a simple camera ontology in OWL:

```
<owl:Class rdf:ID="SLR">
  <rdfs:subClassOf rdf:resource="#Camera"/>
</owl:Class>

<owl:DatatypeProperty rdf:ID="f-stop">
  <rdfs:domain rdf:resource="#Lens"/>
</owl:DatatypeProperty>
```

```
<owl:DatatypeProperty> rdf:ID="aperture">
  <owl:equivalentProperty rdf:resource="#f-stop"/>
</owl:DatatypeProperty>>

<owl:DatatypeProperty rdf:ID="focal-length">
  <rdfs:domain rdf:resource="#Lens"/>
</owl:DatatypeProperty>

<owl:DatatypeProperty> rdf:ID="size">
  <owl:equivalentProperty rdf:resource="#focal-length"/>
</owl:DatatypeProperty>>
```

in other words: SLR is a type of camera, f-stop is synonymous with aperture, and focal length is synonymous with lens size.

Now suppose that an application A is using the second encoding (camera, aperture, lens size), and that it is receiving data from an application B using the first encoding (SLR, f-stop, focal length). As application A parses the XML document that it received from application B, it encounters SLR. It doesn't "understand" SLR so it "consults" the camera ontology: "What do you know about SLR?". The Ontology returns "SLR is a type of Camera". This knowledge provides the link for application A to "understand" the relation between something it doesn't know (SLR) to something it does know (Camera). When application A continues parsing, it encounters f-stop. Again, application A was not coded to understand f-stop, so it consults the camera ontology: "What do you know about f-stop?". The Ontology returns: "f-stop is synonymous with aperture". Once again, this knowledge serves to bridge the terminology gap between something application A doesn't know to something application A does know. And similarly for focal length.

The main point here is that syntactic divergence is no longer a hindrance. In fact, syntactic divergence can be encouraged, so that each application uses the syntactic form that best suits its needs. The ontology provides for a single integration of these different syntactical forms rather $n^2$ individual mappings between the different formats.

Audi is not the only company investigating Semantic Web technology for solving their data integration problems. The same holds for large companies such as Boeing, Daimler Chrysler, Hewlett Packard and others (see Suggested Reading). This application scenario is now realistic enough that companies like Unicorn (Israel), Ontoprise (Germany), Network Inference (UK) and others world-wide are staking their business interests on this use of Semantic Web technology.

## 6.4   Skill Finding at Swiss Life

### 6.4.1   The Setting

Swiss Life is one of Europe's leading life insurers, with 11,000 employees world wide, and some $14 billion of written premiums. Swiss Life has subsidiaries, branches, representative offices, and partners representing its interests in about fifty different countries.

The tacit knowledge, personal competencies, and skills of its employees are the most important resources of any company for solving knowledge-intensive tasks; they are the real substance of the company's success. Establishing an electronically accessible repository of people's capabilities, experiences, and key knowledge areas is one of the major building blocks in setting up enterprise knowledge management. Such a skills repository can be used to enable a search for people with specific skills, expose skill gaps and competency levels, direct training as part of career planning, and document the company's intellectual capital.

### 6.4.2   The Problem

With such a large and international workforce, distributed over many geographical and culturally diverse areas, the construction of a company-wide skills repository is a difficult task. How to list the large number of different skills? How to organise them so that they can be retrieved across geographical and cultural boundaries? How to ensure that the repository is updated frequently?

### 6.4.3   The Contribution of Semantic Web Technology

The experiment at Swiss Life performed in the On-To-Knowledge project (see Suggested Reading) used a hand -built ontology to cover skills in three organizational units of Swiss Life: Information Technology, Private Insurance and Human Resources. Across these three sections, the ontology consisted of 700 concepts, with an additional 180 educational concepts and 130 job function concepts that were not subdivided across the three domains.

Here, we give a glimpse of part of the ontology, to give a flavor of the kind of expressivity that was used:

```
<owl:Class rdf:ID="Skills">
 <rdfs:subClassOf>
  <owl:Restriction>
   <owl:onProperty rdf:resource="#HasSkillsLevel"/>
   <owl:cardinality rdf:datatype="&xsd;nonNegativeInteger">
    1
   </owl:cardinality>
   </owl:Restriction>
 </rdfs:subClassOf>
</owl:Class>

<owl:ObjectProperty rdf:ID="HasSkills">
 <rdfs:domain rdf:resource="#Employee"/>
 <rdfs:range  rdf:resource="#Skills"/>
</owl:ObjectProperty>

<owl:ObjectProperty rdf:ID="WorksInProject">
 <rdfs:domain rdf:resource="#Employee"/>
 <rdfs:range  rdf:resource="#Project"/>
 <owl:inverseOf rdf:resource="#ProjectMembers"/>
</owl:ObjectProperty>

<owl:ObjectProperty rdf:ID="ManagementLevel">
 <rdfs:domain rdf:resource="#Employee"/>
 <rdfs:range>
  <owl:oneOf rdf:parseType="Collection">
   <owl:Thing rdf:about="#member"/>
   <owl:Thing rdf:about="#HeadOfGroup"/>
   <owl:Thing rdf:about="#HeadOfDept"/>
   <owl:Thing rdf:about="#CEO"/>
  </owl:oneOf>
 </rdfs:range>
</owl:ObjectProperty>

<owl:Class rdf:ID="Publishing">
 <rdfs:subClassOf rdf:resource="#Skills"/>
</owl:Class>

<owl:Class rdf:ID="DocumentProcessing">
 <rdfs:subClassOf rdf:resource="#Skills"/>
```

```
</owl:Class>

<owl:Class rdf:ID="DeskTopPublishing">
 <rdfs:subClassOf rdf:resource="#Publishing"/>
 <rdfs:subClassOf rdf:resource="#DocumentProcessing"/>
</owl:Class>
```

Individual employees within Swiss Life were asked to create "home pages" based on form filling that was driven by the skills-ontology. The corresponding collection of instances could be queried using a form-based interface that generated RQL queries (see chapter 3).

Although the system never left the prototype stage, it was in use by initially 100 (later 150) people in selected departments at Swiss Life headquarters.

## 6.5   Think Tank Portal at EnerSearch

### 6.5.1   The Setting

EnerSearch is an industrial research consortium focused on information technology in energy. Its aim is to create and disseminate knowledge on how the use of advanced IT will impact on the energy utility sector, particularly in view of the liberalization of this sector across Europe.

EnerSearch has a structure that is very different from a traditional research company. Research projects are carried out by a varied and changing group of researchers spread over different countries (Sweden, United States, the Netherlands, Germany, France). Many of them, although funded for their work, are not employees of EnerSearch. Thus, EnerSearch is organized as a virtual organization. The insights derived from the conducted research are intended for interested utility industries and IT suppliers. Here, EnerSearch has the structure of a limited company, which is owned by a number of firms in the industry sector that have an express interest in the research being carried out. Shareholding companies include large utility companies in different European countries, including Sweden (Sydkraft), Portugal (EDP), the Netherlands (ENECO), Spain (Iberdrola) and Germany (Eon), as well as some worldwide IT suppliers to this sector (IBM, ABB). Because of this wide geographical spread, EnerSearch also has the character of a virtual organization from a knowledge distribution point of view.

### 6.5.2   The Problem

Dissemination of knowledge is a key function of EnerSearch. The EnerSearch web site is an important mechanism for knowledge dissemination. (In fact, one of the shareholding companies actually entered EnerSearch directly as a result of getting to know the web site). Nevertheless, the information structure of the web site leaves much to be desired. Its main organization is in terms of "about us" information: what projects have been done, which researchers are involved, papers, reports and presentations. Consequently, it does not satisfy the needs of information seekers. They are generally not interested in knowing what the projects are, or who the authors are, but rather in finding answers to questions that are important in this industry domain, such as: does load management lead to cost-saving? If so, how big are they, and what are the required upfront investments? Can powerline communication be technically competitive to ADSL or cable modems?

### 6.5.3   The Contribution of Semantic Web Technology

The EnerSearch web-site is in fact used by different target groups: researchers in the field, staff and management of utility industries, and so on. It is quite possible to form a clear picture of what kind of topics and questions would be relevant for these target groups. Finally, the knowledge domain in which EnerSearch works is relatively well defined. As a result of these factors, it is possible to define a domain ontology that is sufficiently stable and of good enough quality. In fact, the On-To-Knowledge project ran successful experiments using a lightweight "EnerSearch lunchtime ontology" that took developers no more than a few hours to develop (over lunchtime).

This lightweight ontology consisted only of a taxonomical hierarchy (and therefore only needed RDF Schema expressivity). The following is a snapshot of one of the branches of this ontology in informal notation:

```
  ...
    IT
      Hardware
      Software
      Applications
      Communication
        Powerline
        Agent
      Electronic Commerce
      Agents
```

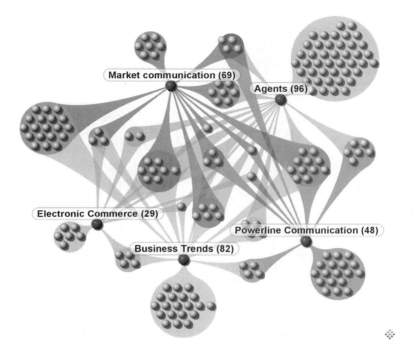

**Figure 6.2**   Semantic map of part of the EnerSearch Web site

```
Multi-agent systems
Intelligent agents
Market/auction
Resource allocation
Algorithms
```

This ontology was used in a number of different ways to drive navigation tools on the EnerSearch web site. Figure 6.2 shows a semantic map of the EnerSearch web site for the subtopics of the concept "agent" and figure 6.3 shows the semantic distance between different authors, in terms of their disciplinary fields of research and publication.[5]

Figure 6.4 shows how some of the same information is displayed to the user in an entirely different manner with the Spectacle Server semantic

5. Both figures display results obtained by using semantic clustering visualization software from Aduna, <http://www.aduna.biz>.

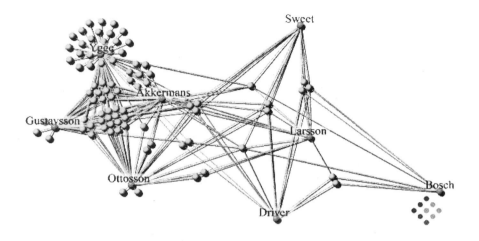

**Figure 6.3**   Semantic distance between EnerSearch authors

browsing software.[6] The user selected the "By Author" option, then chose the author Fredrik Ygge and the concept "cable length". The result lists all the pages with publication on this topic by Fredrik Ygge.

A third way of displaying the information was created by the QuizRDF tool[7]. Rather then choosing between either an entirely ontology based display (as in the three displayed figures), or a traditional keyword based search without any semantic grounding, QuizRDF aims to combine both: the user can type in general keywords. This will result in a traditional list of papers containing these keywords. However, it also displays those concepts in the hierarchy which describe these papers, allowing the user to embark on an ontology-driven search starting from the hits that resulted from a keyword-based search.

In this application scenario we have seen how a traditional information source can be disclosed in a number of innovative ways. All these disclosure mechanisms (textual and graphic, searching or browsing) are based on a single underlying lightweight ontology but cater for a broad spectrum of users with different needs and backgrounds.

6. From Aduna, <http://www.aduna.biz>.
7. Prototyped by British Telecom Research Labs.

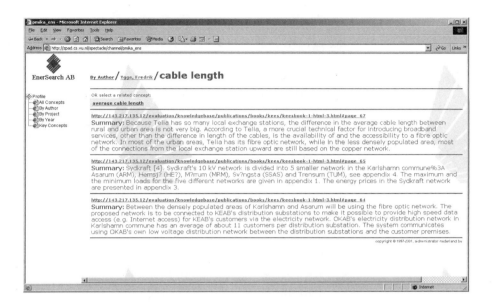

**Figure 6.4**   Browsing ontologically organized papers in Spectacle

## 6.6   e-Learning

### 6.6.1   The Setting

The World Wide Web is currently changing many areas of human activity, among them learning. Traditionally learning has been characterized by the following properties:

- Educator-driven. The instructor selects the content and the pedagogical means of delivery, and sets the agenda and the pace of learning.

- Linear access. Knowledge is taught in a predetermined order. The learner is not supposed to deviate from this order by selecting pieces of particular interest.

- Time- and locality-dependent. Learning takes place at specific times and specific places.

As a consequence, learning has not been personalized but rather aimed at mass participation. Though efficient and in many instances effective, traditional learning processes have not been suitable for every potential learner. The emergence of the Internet has paved the way for implementing new educational processes.

The changes are already visible in higher education. Increasingly, universities are refocusing their activities to provide more flexibility for learners. Virtual universities and online courses are only a small part of these activities. Flexibility and new educational means are also implemented on traditional campuses, where students' presence is still required but with fewer constraints. Increasingly, students can make choices, determine the content and evaluation procedures, the pace of their learning, and the learning method most suitable for them.

We can calso expect e-learning to have an even greater impact on work-related qualifications and life long learning activities. One of the critical support mechanisms for increasing an organization's competitiveness is the improvement of the skills of its employees. Organizations require learning processes that are just-in-time, tailored to their specific needs, and ideally integrated into day-to-day work patterns. These requirements are not compatible with traditional learning, but e-learning shows great promise for addressing these concerns.

### 6.6.2  The Problem

Compared to traditional learning, e-learning is not driven by the instructor. In particular, learners can access material in an order that is not predefined, and can compose individual courses by selecting educational material. For this approach to work, learning material must be equipped with additional information to support effective indexing and retrieval.

The use of metadata is a natural answer and has been followed, in a limited way, by librarians for a long time. In the e-learning community, standards such as IEEE LOM have emerged. They associate with learning materials information, such as educational and pedagogical properties, access rights and conditions of use, and relations to other educational resources. Although these standards are useful, they suffer from a drawback common to all solutions based solely on metadata (XML-like approaches): lack of semantics. As a consequence combining of materials by different authors may be difficult; retrieval may not be optimally supported; and the retrieval and organization of learning resources must be made manually (instead of, say, by a personalized automated agent). These kinds of problems may be avoided if the Semantic Web approach is adopted.

### 6.6.3   The Contribution of Semantic Web Technology

The key ideas of the Semantic Web, namely, common shared meaning (ontology) and machine-processable metadata, establish a promising approach for satisfying the e-learning requirements. It can support both semantic querying and the conceptual navigation of learning materials.

- Learner-driven. Learning materials, possibly by different authors, can be linked to commonly agreed ontologies. Personalized courses can be designed through semantic querying, and learning materials can be retrieved in the context of actual problems, as decided by the learner.

- Flexible access. Knowledge can be accessed in any order the learner wishes, according to her interests and needs. Of course, appropriate semantic annotation will still set constraints in cases where prerequisites are necessary. But overall nonlinear access will be supported.

- Integration. The Semantic Web can provide a uniform platform for the business processes of organizations, and learning activities can be integrated in these processes. This solution may be particularly valuable for commercial companies.

### 6.6.4   Ontologies for e-Learning

In an e-learning environment the situation can easily arise that different authors use different terminologies, in which case the combination of learning materials becomes difficult. The retrieval problem is additionally compounded by the fact that typically instructors and learners have very different backgrounds and levels of knowledge. Therefore, some mechanism for establishing a shared understanding is needed. Ontologies are a powerful mechanism for achieving this task. In an e-learning environment it makes sense to distinguish between three types of knowledge, and thus of ontologies: content, pedagogy, and structure.

A *content ontology* describes the basic concepts of the domain in which learning takes place (e.g., history or computer science). It includes also the relations between these concepts, and some basic properties. For example, the study of Classical Athens is part of the history of Ancient Greece, which in turn is part of Ancient History. The ontology should include the relation "is part of" and the fact that it is transitive (e.g., expressed in OWL). In this way, an automated learning support agent can infer that knowledge on Classical Athens can be found under Ancient History. The content ontology can also use relations to capture synonyms, abbreviations, and so on.

Pedagogical issues can be addressed in a *pedagogy ontology*. For example, material can be classified as lecture, tutorial, example, walk-through, exercise, solution, and so on. Finally, a *structure ontology* is used to define the logical structure of the learning materials. Typical knowledge of this kind includes hierarchical and navigational relations like *previous, next, hasPart, isPartOf, requires,* and *isBasedOn*. Relationships between these relations can also be defined; for example, *hasPart* and *isPartOf* are inverse relations. It is natural to develop e-learning systems on the Web; thus a Web ontology language should be used.

We should mention that most of the inferences drawn from learning ontologies cannot be expected to be very deep. Human readers can easily deal with relations such as *hasPart* and *isPartOf* and their interplay. The point is, though, that this kind of reasoning should be exhibited by *automated agents*, and the semantic information is necessary for reasoning to occur in an automated fashion.

## 6.7   Web Services

### 6.7.1   The Setting

By web services we mean Web sites that do not merely provide static information, but involve interaction with users and often allow users to effect some action. Usually a distinction is made between simple and complex Web services.

Simple Web services involve a single Web-accessible program, sensor, or device that does not rely upon other Web services nor requires further interaction with the user, beyond a simple response. Typical examples are information provision services, such as a flight finder and a service that returns the postal code of a given address.

Complex Web services are composed of simpler services, and often require ongoing interaction with the user, whereby the user can make choices or provide information conditionally. For example, user interaction with an online music store involves searching for CDs and titles by various criteria, reading reviews and listening to samples, adding CDs to a shopping cart, providing credit card details, shipping details, and delivery address.

## 6.7.2   The Problem and the Contribution of Semantic Web Technology

At present, the use of Web services requires human involvement. For example, information has to be browsed and forms need to be filled in. The Semantic Web vision, as applied to Web services, aims at automating the discovery, invocation, composition and monitoring of Web services by providing machine-interpretable descriptions of services.

Web sites should be able to employ a set of basic classes and properties by declaring and describing services, an *ontology of services*. DAML-S is an initiative that is developing an ontology language for Web services. It makes use of DAML+OIL, that is, it can be viewed as a layer on top of DAML+OIL (a DAML+OIL application). Currently DAML-S is very much under development (among other things DAML-S is migrated to OWL), so we will refrain from providing technical details, and will concentrate on the basic ideas instead.

There are three basic kinds of knowledge associated with a service: *service profiles, service models, and service groundings*.

A service profile is a description of the offerings and requirements of a service, in a sense, its specification. This information is essential for a *service discovery*: a service-seeking agent can determine whether a service is appropriate for its purposes, based on the service profile. It is also interesting to note that a service profile may not be a description of an existing service but rather a specification of a needed service, provided by a service requester.

A service model describes how a service works, that is, what exactly happens when the service is carried out. Such information may be important for a service-seeking agent for composing services to perform a complex task, and for monitoring the execution of the service.

A service grounding specifies details of how an agent can access a service. Typically a grounding will specify a communication protocol and port numbers to be used in contacting the service.

In the following we briefly discuss service profiles and service models in DAML-S.

### Service Profiles

Service profiles provide a way to describe services offered by a Web site but also services needed by requesters. This way, matching of requests and offerings is supported. In general, a service profile in DAML-S provides the following information:

- A human-readable description of the service and its provider

- A specification of the functionalities provided by the service

- Additional information, such as expected response time and geographic constraints.

All this information is encoded in the modelling primitives of DAML-S: DAML-S classes and properties, which in turn are defined using the DAML+OIL language. For example, an offering of a service is an instance of the class `OfferedService`, which is defined as follows:

```
<rdfs:Class rdf:ID="OfferedService">
    <rdfs:label>OfferedService</rdfs:label>
    <rdfs:subClassOf rdf:resource= "http://www.daml.org/
        services/daml-s/2001/10/Service.daml#"/>
</rdfs:Class>
```

A number of properties are defined on this class: `intendedPurpose`, `serviceName`, and `providedBy`. The range of the first two properties comprises strings, and the range of the third property is a new class, `Service-Provider`, which has various properties. Here is a simple example of an instance:

```
<profile:ServiceProvider rdf:ID="SportsNews">
    <profile:phone>1234 5678</profile:phone>
    <profile:fax>1234 5679</profile:fax>
    <profile:email>abc@defgh.com</profile:email>
    <profile:webURL>www.defgh.com</profile:webURL>
    <profile:physicalAddress>150 Nowhere St,
        111 Somewhere, Australia</profile:PhysicalAddress>
</profile:ServiceProvider>
```

The functional description of a service profile defines properties describing the functionality provided by the service. The main properties are

input  which describes the parameters necessary for providing the service. For example, a sports news service might require the following input: date, sports category, customer credit card details.

output  which specifies the outputs of the service. In the sports news example, the output would be the news articles in the specified category at the given date.

`precondition` which specifies the conditions that need to hold for the
service to be provided effectively. The distinction between inputs and
preconditions can be illustrated in our running example: the credit card
details are an input, and preconditions are that the credit card is valid and
not overcharged.

`effect,` a property that specifies the effects of the service. In our example,
an effect might be that the credit card is charged $1 per news article.

At present, the modelling primitives of DAML-S are very limited regarding
the functional description of services, because of limitations of the underlying DAML+OIL language. (These same limitations apply to OWL). For
example, it is not possible to define logical relationships between inputs and
outputs, as one would do in, say, software specification. The developers
of DAML-S intend to provide such possibilities once the Web ontology language is augmented by logical capabilities, e.g., rules.

**Service Models**

Service models are based on the key concept of a *process*, which describes
a service in terms of inputs, outputs, preconditions, effects, and where appropriate, its composition of component subprocesses. We have already discussed inputs, outputs, preconditions, and effects for the profile model, so
here we concentrate on the composition of a complex process from simpler
processes.

Figure 6.5 shows the top level of the process ontology. We see the top class
`Process` with its three subclasses:

- *Atomic processes* can be directly invoked by passing them appropriate mes-
  sages; they execute in one step.

- *Simple processes* are elements of abstraction; they can be thought of as having single-step executions but are not invocable.

- *Composite processes* consist of other, simpler processes.

Let us describe a few properties shown in figure 6.5.

- `hasProfile` and `hasProcess` are two properties that state the relationship between a process and its profile.

- A simple process may be *realized* by an atomic process.

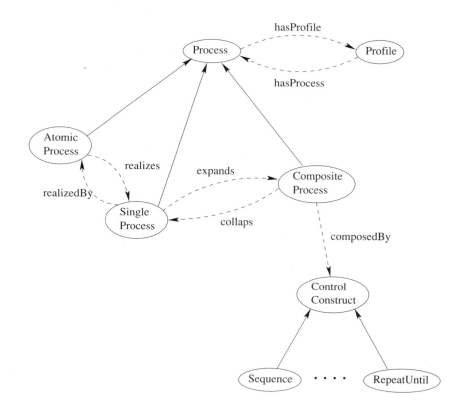

**Figure 6.5**   Top level of the process ontology

- Alternatively, it is used for abstraction purposes and *expands* to a composite process.

Finally, a composite process is composed of a number of *control constructs*:

```
<rdf:Property rdf:ID="composedBy">
    <rdfs:domain rdf:resource="#CompositeProcess"/>
    <rdfs:range rdf:resource="#ControlConstruct"/>
</rdf:Property>
```

The control constructs currently offered by DAML-S include, sequence, choice, if-then-else and repeat-until.

As for service profiles, the process model of DAML-S is still under development.

**AI and Web Services**

Web services are an application area where Artificial Intelligence techniques can be used effectively, for instance, for matching between service offers and service requests, and for composing complex services from simpler services, where automated planning can be utilized. A few links to relevant references are found in the Suggested Reading.

## 6.8   Other Scenarios

In this section, we mention in somewhat less detail a number of other application scenarios that are being pursued in various sectors of industry or research.

### 6.8.1   Multimedia Collection Indexing at Scotland Yard

Special sections of police forces such as Scotland Yard and Interpol are concerned with theft of art and antique objects. It is often hard enough to track down the perpetrators of such thefts, but even when this has been successfully done, and when some of the stolen artifacts have been recovered, it turns out to be a surprisingly hard problem to return the objects to their original owners. Even though international databases of stolen art objects exist, it is difficult to locate specific objects in these databases, because different parties are likely to offer different descriptions. A museum reporting a theft may describe an object as "a Song dynasty Ying Ging lotus vase", whereas a police officer reporting a recovered item may simply enter a "12.5 inch high pale green vase with floral designs". It currently takes human experts to recognize that the vase entered as stolen is indeed the same one reported as recovered.

   Part of the solution is to develop controlled vocabularies such as the Art and Architecture Thesaurus (AAT) from the Getty Trust,[8] or Iconclass thesaurus[9] to extend them into full-blown ontologies, to develop software that can automatically recognize classified objects from descriptions of their physical appearance using ontological background knowledge, and to deal with the ontology-mapping problem that exists when different parties have described the same artifacts using different ontologies.

---

8. <http://www.getty.edu/research/tools/vocabulary/aat>.
9. <http://www.iconclass.nl/>.

### 6.8.2    Online Procurement at Daimler-Chrysler

Like all car-manufacturing companies today, Daimler-Chrysler interacts with
hundreds of suppliers in order to obtain all the parts that go into making
a single car.  In recent years, online procurement has been identified as a
major potential cost saver, for instance the paper-based process of exchanging contracts, orders, invoices, and money transfers can be replaced by an
electronic process of data-interchange between software applications.  Also,
static, long-term agreements with a fixed set of suppliers can be replaced by
dynamic, short-term agreements in a competitive open marketplace.  Whenever a supplier is offering a better deal, Daimler-Chrysler wants to be able to
switch rather then being locked into a long-term arrangement with another
supplier.

This online procurement is one of the major drivers behind business-to-
business (B2B) e-commerce.  Current efforts in B2B e-commerce rely heavily on a priori standardization of data formats, that is, off-line industrywide
agreements on data formats and their intended semantics.  Organizations
such as Rosetta Net[10] are dedicated to such standardization efforts. To quote
from RosettaNet's Web site:

> RosettaNet [is] a self-funded, non-profit organization. [It] is a consor-
> tium of major Information Technology, Electronic Components, Semi-
> conductor Manufacturing, and Telecommunications companies work-
> ing to create and implement industrywide, open e-business process
> standards.  These standards form a common e-business language,
> aligning processes between supply chain partners on a global basis.

Since such data formats are specified in XML, no semantics can be read from
the file alone, and partners must agree in time-consuming and expensive
standards negotiations, followed by hard-coding the intended semantics of
the data format into their code.

A more attractive road would use formats such as RDF Schema and OWL,
with their explicitly defined formal semantics. This would make product descriptions "carry their semantics on their sleeve," opening the way for much
more liberal online B2B procurement processes than currently possible.

---

10. <http://www.rosettanet.org>.

### 6.8.3  Device interoperability at Nokia

(This section is based on a use-case from the OWL Requirements document; see Suggested Reading section.) Recent years have seen an explosive proliferation of digital devices in our daily environment: PDAs, mobile telephones, digital cameras, laptops, wireless access in public locations, GPS-enabled cars. Given this proliferation, interoperability among these devices is becoming highly desirable. The pervasiveness and the wireless nature of these devices require network architectures to support automatic, ad hoc configuration.

A key technology of true ad hoc networks is service discovery, functionality by which services (functions offered by various devices such as cell phones, printers and sensors) can be described, advertised, and discovered by others. All current service discovery and capability description mechanisms (e.g., Sun's JINI, Microsoft's UPnP) are based on ad hoc representation schemes and rely heavily on standardization (on a priori identification of all those things one would want to communicate or discuss).

More attractive than this a priori standardization is "serendipitous interoperability," interoperability under "unchoreographed" conditions, that is, devices that are not necessarily designed to work together (such as ones built for different purposes, by different manufacturers, at a different time) should be able to discover each others' functionality and be able to take advantage of it. Being able to "understand" other devices and reason about their services/functionality is necessary, because full-blown ubiquitous computing scenarios involve dozens if not hundreds of devices, and a priori standardization of the usage scenarios is an unmanageable task.

Similar to the scenario of online procurement, ontologies (with their standardized semantics) are required to make such "unchoreographed" understanding of functionalities possible.

## Suggested Reading

A nontechnical book on the use of ontologies in electronic commerce and knowledge management:

- D. Fensel. *Ontologies: A Silver Bullet for Knowledge Management and Electronic Commerce.* New York: Springer 2001.

The use-case document for OWL describes a number of use-cases that motivated the W3C's Web Ontology Working Group in defining OWL:

- J. Heflin. OWL Web Ontology Language Use Cases and Requirements. August 18, 2003.<http://www.w3.org/TR/webont-req/>.

The following book describes three different application case-studies that were performed in the On-To-Knowledge project. More information on this project can also be found at <http://www.ontoknowledge.org>.

- J. Davies, D. Fensel, and F. van Harmelen. *Towards the Semantic Web: Ontology-Driven Knowledge Management*. New York: Wiley, 2003.

A collection of papers on industrial applications of Semantic Web technology can be found in the Industrial Track papers of the International Semantic Web Conferences, starting from the 2003 conference:

- D. Fensel, K. Sycara, J. Mylopoulos, eds. *Proceedings of the 2nd International Semantic Web Conference*. New York. Springer, 2003. Lecture Notes in Computer Science, volume 2870.

A paper describing the potential benefits of the Semantic Web for e-learning:

- L. Stojanovic, S. Staab and R. Studer. eLearning Based on the Semantic Web. In *Proceedings of WebNet 2001 - World Conference on the WWW and the Internet*. <http://www.aifb.uni-karlsruhe.de/WBS/Publ/2001/ WebNet_lstsstrst_2001.pdf>

Two relevant references for Semantic Web portal applications:

- S. Staab et al. Semantic Community Web Portals. In *Proceedings of the 9th International WWW Conference*. 2000 <http://www9.org/w9cdrom/134/134.html>

- N. Stojanovic et al. SEAL – A Framework for Developing SEmantic PortALs. In *Proceedings of the 1st International Conference on Knowledge Capture (K-CAP)*. 2001. <http://www.aifb.uni-karlsruhe.de/WBS/Publ/2001/sealkcap2.pdf>

The main page on DAML-S and DAML-enabled Web services is

- <http://www.daml.org/services/>

Some relevant publications:

- The DAML Services Coalition. DAML-S: Web Service Description for the Semantic Web. In *Proceedings of the 1st International Semantic Web Conference (ISWC)*. New York: Springer 2002. Lecture Notes in AI Volume 2342. <http://www.daml.org/services/ISWC2002-DAMLS.pdf>

- M. Paolucci et al. Semantic Matching of Web Services Capabilities. In *Proceedings of the 1st International Semantic Web Conference (ISWC)*. New York: Springer 2002. Lecture Notes in AI Volume 2342. <http://www.daml.org/services/ISWC2002-Matchmaker.pdf>

- S. McIlraith, T.C. Son, and H. Zeng. Mobilizing the Semantic Web with DAML-Enabled Web Services. In *Proceedings of the 2nd International Workshop on the Semantic Web (SemWeb 2001)*. <http://www.daml.org/services/SemWeb01-KSL.pdf>

Some useful websites with collections of tools are:

<http://business.semanticweb.org>. A very good resource on the use of Semantic Web technolgy in companies, and a list of providers of Semantic Web technology.

<http://www.daml.org/tools> is an extensive repository of tools. Although at present, these are for DAML+OIL, but many are exptected to be upgraded to OWL.

<http://www.w3.org/2001/sw/WebOnt/impls#Implementations> and

<http://www.cs.man.ac.uk/~horrocks/OntoWeb/SIG/node3.html> is a list of the first tools that came out after the OWL specification stabilized.

<http://www.ilrt.bris.ac.uk/discovery/rdf/resources/>. Tools, projects, and applications for RDF and RDF Schema.

# 7 *Ontology Engineering*

## 7.1   Introduction

In this book, we have focused mainly on the techniques that are essential to the Semantic Web: representation languages, query languages, transformation and inference techniques, tools. Clearly, the introduction of such a large volume of new tools and techniques also raises methodological questions: how can tools and techniques best be appliled? Which languages and tools should be used in which circumstances, and in which order? What about issues of quality control and resource management?

Many of these questions for the Semantic Web have been studied in other contexts, for example in software engineering, object-oriented design, and knowledge engineering. It is beyond the scope of this book to give a comprehensive treatment of all of these issues. Nevertheless, in this chapter, we briefly discuss some of the methodological issues that arise when building ontologies, in particular, constructing ontologies manually, reusing existing ontologies, and using semiautomatic methods.

## 7.2   Constructing Ontologies Manually

For our discussion of the manual construction of ontologies, we follow mainly Noy and McGuinness, "Ontology Development 101: A Guide to Creating Your First Ontology." Further references are provided in Suggested Reading.

We can distinguish the following main stages in the ontology development process:

1. Determine scope.   5. Define properties.
2. Consider reuse.     6. Define facets.
3. Enumerate terms.   7. Define instances.
4. Define taxonomy.   8. Check for anomalies.

Like any development process, this is in practice not a linear process. These above steps will have to be iterated, and backtracking to earlier steps may be necessary at any point in the process. We will not further discuss this complex process management. Instead, we turn to the individual steps:

### 7.2.1   Determine Scope

Developing an ontology of the domain is not a goal in itself. Developing an ontology is akin to defining a set of data and their structure for other programs to use. In other words, an ontology is a *model* of a particular domain, built for a particular purpose. As a consequence, there is no *correct* ontology of a specific domain. An ontology is by necessity an abstraction of a particular domain, and there are always viable alternatives. What is included in this abstraction should be determined by the use to which the ontology will be put, and by future extensions that are already anticipated. Basic questions to be answered at this stage are: What is the domain that the ontology will cover? For what we are going to use the ontology? For what types of questions should the ontology provide answers? Who will use and maintain the ontology?

### 7.2.2   Consider Reuse

With the spreading deployment of the Semantic Web, ontologies will become more widely available. Already we rarely have to start from scratch when defining an ontology. There is almost always an ontology available from a third party that provides at least a useful starting point for our own ontology. (See section 7.3).

### 7.2.3   Enumerate Terms

A first step toward the actual definition of the ontology is to write down in an unstructured list all the relevant terms that are expected to appear in the ontology. Typically, nouns form the basis for class names, and verbs (or verb phrases) form the basis for property names (for example, *is part of*, *has component*).

Traditional knowledge engineering tools such as laddering and grid analysis can be productively used in this stage to obtain both the set of terms and an initial structure for these terms.

### 7.2.4   Define Taxonomy

After the identification of relevant terms, these terms must be organized in a taxonomic hierarchy. Opinions differ on whether it is more efficient/reliable to do this in a top-down or a bottom-up fashion.

It is, of course, important to ensure that the hierarchy is indeed a taxonomic (subclass) hierarchy. In other words, if A is a subclass of B, then every instance of A must also be an instance of B. Only this will ensure that we respect the built-in semantics of primitives such as `owl:subClassOf` and `rdfs:subClassOf`.

### 7.2.5   Define Properties

This step is often interleaved with the previous one: it is natural to organize the properties that link the classes while organizing these classes in a hierarchy.

Remember that the semantics of the `subClassOf` relation demands that whenever A is a subclass of B, every property statement that holds for instances of B must also apply to instances of A. Because of this inheritance, it makes sense to attach properties to the highest class in the hierarchy to which they apply.

While attaching properties to classes, it makes sense to immediately provide statements about the domain and range of these properties. There is a methodological tension here between generality and specificity. On the one hand, it is attractive to give properties as general a domain and range as possible, enabling the properties to be used (through inheritance) by subclasses. On the other hand, it is useful to define domains and range as narrowly as possible, enabling us to detect potential inconsistencies and misconceptions in the ontology by spotting domain and range violations.

### 7.2.6   Define Facets

It is interesting to note that after all these steps, the ontology will only require the expressivity provided by RDF Schema and does not use any of the additional primitives in OWL. This will change in the current step, that of enriching the previously defined properties with facets:

- Cardinality. Specify for as many properties as possible whether they are allowed or required to have a certain number of different values. Often, occurring cases are "at least one value" (i.e., required properties) and "at most one value" (i.e., single-valued properties).

- Required values. Often, classes are defined by virtue of a certain property's having particular values, and such required values can be specified in OWL, using `owl:hasValue`. Sometimes the requirements are less stringent: a property is required to have some values from a given class (and not necessarily a specific value, `owl:someValuesFrom`).

- Relational characteristics. The final family of facets concerns the relational characteristics of properties: symmetry, transitivity, inverse properties, functional values.

After this step in the ontology construction process, it will be possible to check the ontology for internal inconsistencies. (This is not possible before this step, simply because RDF Schema is not rich enough to express inconsistencies). Examples of often occurring inconsistencies are incompatible domain and range definitions for transitive, symmetric, or inverse properties. Similarly, cardinality properties are frequent sources of inconsistencies. Finally, requirements on property values can conflict with domain and range restrictions, giving yet another source of possible inconsistencies.

### 7.2.7   Define Instances

Of course, we do rarely define ontologies for their own sake. Instead we use ontologies to organize sets instances, and it is a separate step to fill the ontologies with such intances. Typically, the number of instances is many orders of magnitude larger then the number of classes from the ontology. Ontologies vary in size from a few hundred classes to tens of thousands of classes; the number of instances varies from hundreds to hundreds of thousands, or even larger.

Because of these large numbers, populating an ontology with instances is typically not done manually. Often, instances are retrieved from legacy datasources such as databases. Another often used technique is the automated extraction of instances from a text corpus.

### 7.2.8 Check for Anomalies

An important advantage of the use of OWL over RDF Schema is the possibility to detect inconsistencies in the ontology itself, or in the set of instances that were defined to populate the ontology. Some examples of often occurring anomalies are the following: As mentioned above, examples of often occurring inconsistencies are incompatible domain and range definitions for transitive, symmetric, or inverse properties. Similarly, cardinality properties are frequent sources of inconsistencies. Finally, the requirements on property values can conflict with domain and range restrictions, giving yet another source of possible inconsistencies.

## 7.3 Reusing Existing Ontologies

One should begin with an existing ontology if possible. Existing ontologies come in a wide variety.

### 7.3.1 Codified Bodies of Expert Knowledge

Some ontologies are carefully crafted, by a large team of experts over many years. An example in the medical domain is the cancer ontology from the National Cancer Institute in the United States.[1] Examples in the cultural domain are the Art and Architecture Thesaurus (AAT)[2] containing 125,000 terms and the Union List of Artist Names (ULAN),[3] with 220,000 entries on artists. Another example is the Iconclass vocabulary of 28,000 terms for describing cultural images.[4] An example from the geographical domain is the Getty Thesaurus of Geographic Names (TGN),[5] containing over 1 million entries.

### 7.3.2 Integrated Vocabularies

Sometimes attempts have been made to merge a number of independently developed vocabularies into a single large resource. The prime example of this is the Unified Medical Language System,[6] which integrates 100 biomed-

---

1. <http://www.mindswap.org/2003/CancerOntology/>.
2. <http://www.getty.edu/research/tools/vocabulary/aat>.
3. <http://www.getty.edu/research/conducting_research/vocabularies/ulan/>.
4. <http://www.iconclass.nl>.
5. <http://www.getty.edu/research/conducting_research/vocabularies/tgn/>.
6. <http://umlsinfo.nlm.nih.gov>.

ical vocabularies and classifications. The UMLS metathesaurus alone contains 750,000 concepts, with over 10 million links between them. Not surprisingly, the semantics of such a resource that integrates many independently developed vocabularies is rather low, but nevertheless it has turned out to be very useful in many applications, at least as a starting point.

### 7.3.3   Upper-Level Ontologies

Whereas the preceding ontologies are all highly domain-specific, some attempts have been made to define very generally applicable ontologies (sometimes known as upper-level ontologies). The two prime examples are Cyc,[7] with 60,000 assertions on 6,000 concepts, and the Standard Upperlevel Ontology (SUO).[8]

### 7.3.4   Topic Hierarchies

Other "ontologies" hardly deserve this name in a strict sense: they are simply sets of terms, loosely organized in a specialization hierarchy. This hierarchy is typically not a strict taxonomy but rather mixes different specialization relations, such as *is-a*, *part-of*, *contained-in*. Nevertheless, such resources are often very useful as a starting point. A large example is the Open Directory hierarchy[9], containing more then 400,000 hierarchically organized categories and available in RDF format.

### 7.3.5   Linguistic Resources

Some resources were originally built not as abstractions of a particular domain, but rather as linguistic resources. Again, these have been shown to be useful as starting places for ontology development. The prime example in this category is WordNet, with over 90,000 word senses.[10]

### 7.3.6   Ontology Libraries

Attempts are currently underway to construct online libraries of online ontologies. Examples may be found at the Ontology Engineering Group's Web

---

7. <http://www.opencyc.org/>.
8. <http://suo.ieee.org/>.
9. <http://dmoz.org>.
10. <http://www.cogsci.princeton.edu/~wn>, available in RDF at <http://www.semanticweb.org/library/>.

site[11] and at the DAML Web site.[12] Work on XML Schema development, although strictly speaking not ontologies, may also be a useful starting point for development work.[13]

It is rarely the case that existing ontologies can be reused without changes. Typically, existing concepts and properties must be refined (using `owl:subClassOf` and `owl:subPropertyOf`). Also, alternative names must be introduced which are better suited to the particular domain (for example, using `owl:equivalentClass` and `owl:equivalentProperty`). Also, this is an opportunity for fruitfully exploiting the fact that RDF and OWL allow private refinements of classes defined in other ontologies.

The general question of importing ontologies and establishing mappings between different mappings is still wide open, and is considered to be one of the hardest (and most urgent) Semantic Web research issues.

## 7.4 Using Semiautomatic Methods

There are two core challenges for putting the vision of the Semantic Web into action.

First, one has to support the re-engineering task of semantic enrichment for building the Web of meta-data. The success of the Semantic Web greatly depends on the proliferation of ontologies and relational metadata. This requires that such metadata can be produced at high speed and low cost. To this end, the task of merging and aligning ontologies for establishing semantic interoperability may be supported by machine learning techniques

Second, one has to provide a means for maintaining and adopting the machine-processable data that is the basic for the Semantic Web. Thus, we need mechanisms that support the dynamic nature of the Web.

Although ontology engineering tools have matured over the last decade, manual ontology acquisition remains a time-consuming, expensive, highly skilled, and sometimes cumbersome task that can easily result in a knowledge acquisition bottleneck.

These problems resemble those that knowledge engineers have dealt with over the last two decades as they worked on knowledge acquisition methodologies or workbenches for defining knowledge bases. The integration of

---

11. <http://www.ontology.or.kr/ontology/onto_lib.asp>.
12. <http://www.daml.org>.
13. See for example the DTD/Schema registry at <http://XML.org> and Rosetta Net <http://www.rosettanet.org>.

knowledge acquisition with machine learning techniques proved beneficial for knowledge acquisition.

The research area of machine learning has a long history, both on knowledge acquisition or extraction and on knowledge revision or maintenance, and it provides a large number of techniques that may be applied to solve these challenges. The following tasks can be supported by machine learning techniques:

- Extraction of ontologies from existing data on the Web

- Extraction of relational data and metadata from existing data on the Web

- Merging and mapping ontologies by analyzing extensions of concepts

- Maintaining ontologies by analyzing instance data

- Improving Semantic Web applications by observing users

Machine learning provides a number of techniques that can be used to support these tasks:

- Clustering

- Incremental ontology updates

- Support for the knowledge engineer

- Improving large natural language ontologies

- Pure (domain) ontology learning

Omalayenko identifies three types of ontologies that can be supported using machine learning techniques and identifies the current state of the art in these areas

### Natural Language Ontologies

Natural language ontologies (NLOs) contain lexical relations between language concepts; they are large in size and do not require frequent updates. Usually they represent the background knowledge of the system and are used to expand user queries The state of the art in NLO learning looks quite optimistic: not only does a stable general-purpose NLO exist but so do techniques for automatically or semiautomatically constructing and enriching domain-specific NLOs.

### Domain Ontologies

Domain ontologies capture knowledge of one particular domain, for instance, pharmacological, or printer knowledge. These ontologies provide a detailed description of the domain concepts from a restricted domain. Usually, they are constructed manually but different learning techniques can assist the (especially inexperienced) knowledge engineer. Learning of the domain ontologies is far less developed than NLO improvement. The acquisition of the domain ontologies is still guided by a human knowledge engineer, and automated learning techniques play a minor role in knowledge acquisition. They have to find statistically valid dependencies in the domain texts and suggest them to the knowledge engineer.

### Ontology Instances

Ontology instances can be generated automatically and frequently updated (e.g., a company profile from the Yellow Pages will be updated frequently) while the ontology remains unchanged. The task of learning of the ontology instances fits nicely into a machine learning framework, and there are several successful applications of machine learning algorithms for this. But these applications are either strictly dependent on the domain ontology or populate the markup without relating to any domain theory. A general-purpose technique for extracting ontology instances from texts given the domain ontology as input has still not been developed.

Besides the different types of ontologies that can be supported, there are also different uses for ontology learning. The first three tasks in the following list (again taken from Omalayenko) relate to ontology acquisition tasks in knowledge engineering, and the last three to ontology maintenance tasks.

- Ontology creation from scratch by the knowledge engineer. In this task machine learning assists the knowledge engineer by suggesting the most important relations in the field or checking and verifying the constructed knowledge bases.

- Ontology schema extraction from Web documents. In this task machine learning systems take the data and metaknowledge (like a metaontology) as input and generate the ready-to-use ontology as output with the possible help of the knowledge engineer.

- Extraction of ontology instances populates given ontology schemas and extracts the instances of the ontology presented in the Web documents.

This task is similar to information extraction and page annotation, and can apply the techniques developed in these areas.

- Ontology integration and navigation deal with reconstructing and navigating in large and possibly machine-learned knowledge bases. For example, the task can be to change the propositional-level knowledge base of the machine learner into a first-order knowledge base.

- An ontology maintenance task is updating some parts of an ontology that are designed to be updated (like formatting tags that have to track the changes made in the page layout).

- Ontology enrichment (or ontology tuning) includes automated modification of minor relations into an existing ontology. This does not change major concepts and structures but makes an ontology more precise.

A wide variety of techniques, algorithms, and tools is available from machine learning. However, an important requirement for ontology representation is that ontologies must be symbolic, human-readable, and understandable. This forces us to deal only with symbolic learning algorithms that make generalizations, and to skip other methods like neural networks and genetic algorithms. Potentially applicable algorithms include

- Propositional rule learning algorithms that learn association rules, or other forms of attribute-value rules.

- Bayesian learning is mostly represented by the Naive Bayes classifier. It is based on the Bayes theorem and generates probabilistic attribute-value rules based on the assumption of conditional independence between the attributes of the training instances.

- First-order logic rules learning induces the rules that contain variables, called first-order Horn clauses.

- Clustering algorithms group the instances together based on the similarity or distance measures between a pair of instances defined in terms of their attribute values.

In conclusion, we can say that although there is much potential for machine learning techniques to be deployed for Semantic Web engineering, this is far from a well-understood area. No off-the-shelf techniques or tools are currently available, although this is likely to change in the near future.

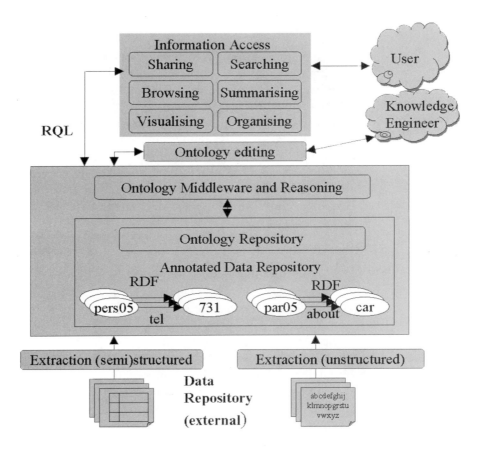

**Figure 7.1**   Semantic Web knowledge management architecture

## 7.5   On-To-Knowledge Semantic Web Architecture

Building the Semantic Web not only involves using the new languages described in this book, but also a rather different style of engineering and a rather different approach to application integration. To illustrate this, we describe in this section how a number of Semantic Web-related tools can be integrated in a single lightweight architecture using Semantic Web standards to achieve interoperability between independently engineered tools (see figure 7.1).

### 7.5.1    Knowledge Acquisition

At the bottom of figure 7.1 we find tools that use surface analysis techniques to obtain content from documents. These can be either unstructured natural language documents or structured and semistructured documents (such as HTML tables and spreadsheets).

In the case of unstructured documents, the tools typically use a combination of statistical techniques and shallow natural language technology to extract key concepts from documents.

In the case of more structured documents, the tools use techniques such as wrappers, induction, and pattern recognition to extract the content from the weak structures found in these documents.

### 7.5.2    Knowledge Storage

The output of the analysis tools is sets of concepts, organized in a shallow concept hierarchy with at best very few cross-taxonomical relationships. RDF and RDF Schema are sufficiently expressive to represent the extracted information.

Besides simply storing the knowledge produced by the extraction tools, the repository must of course provide the ability to retrieve this knowledge, preferably using a structured query language such as discussed in chapter 3. Any reasonable RDF Schema repository will also support the RDF model theory, including deduction of class membership based on domain and range definitions, and deriving the transitive closure of the `subClassOf` relationship.

Note that the repository will store both the ontology (class hierarchy, property definitions) and the instances of the ontology (specific individuals that belong to classes, pairs of individuals between which a specific property holds).

### 7.5.3    Knowledge Maintenance

Besides basic storage and retrieval functionality, a practical Semantic Web repository will have to provide functionality for managing and maintaining the ontology: change management, access and ownership rights, transaction management.

Besides lightweight ontologies that are automatically generated from unstructured and semistructured data, there must be support for human engineering of much more knowledge-intensive ontologies. Sophisticated editing environments must be able to retrieve ontologies from the repository, allow a knowledge engineer to manipulate it, and place it back in the repository.

### 7.5.4    Knowledge Use

The ontologies and data in the repository are to be used by applications that serve an enduser. We have already described a number of such applications.

### 7.5.5    Technical Interoperability

In the On-To-Knowledge project,[14] the architecture of figure 7.1 was implemented with very lightweight connections between the components. Syntactic interoperability was achieved because all components communicated in RDF. Semantic interoperability was achieved because all semantics was expressed using RDF Schema. Physical interoperability was achieved because all communications between components were established using simple HTTP connections, and all but one of the components (the ontology editor) were implemented as remote services. When operating the On-To-Knowledge system from Amsterdam, the ontology extraction tool, running in Norway was given a London-based URL of a document to analyze; the resulting RDF and RDF Schema were uploaded to a repository server running in Amersfoort (the Netherlands). These data were uploaded into a locally installed ontology editor, and after editing downloaded back into the Amersfoort server. The data were then used to drive a Swedish ontology-based Web site generator (see the EnerSearch case-study in chapter 6), as well as a U.K.-based search engine, both displaying their results in the browser on the screen in Amsterdam.

In summary, all these tools were running remotely, were independently engineered, and only relied on HTTP and RDF to obtain a high degree of interoperability.

---

14. <http://www.ontoknowledge.org>.

## Suggested Reading

Some key papers that were used as the basis for this chapter are:

- Ontology Development 101: A Guide to Creating Your First Ontology Natalya. F. Noy and Deborah L. McGuinness
  <http://www.ksl.stanford.edu/people/dlm/papers/ontology101/ontology101-noy-mcguinness.html>.

- M. Uschold, and M. Gruninger. Ontologies: Principles, Methods and Applications. *Knowledge Engineering Review*, Volume 11 Number 2, (June 1996).

- B. Omelayenko. Learning of Ontologies for the Web: the Analysis of Existing Approaches, In: *Proceedings of the International Workshop on Web Dynamics, 8th International Conference on Database Theory (ICDTŠ01)*. 2001.
  <http://www.cs.vu.nl/ borys/papers/WebDyn01.pdf>

Two often cited books are:

- A. Maedche, *Ontology Learning for the Semantic Web*, Kluwer International Series in Engineering and Computer Science, Volume 665, 2002.

- J. Davies, D. Fensel, and F. van Harmelen. *Towards the Semantic Web: Ontology-Driven Knowledge Management*. New York: Wiley, 2003.

## Project

This project is a mediumscale exercise that will occupy two or three people for about two to three weeks. All required software is freely available. We provide some pointers to software that we have used successfully, but given the very active state of development of the field, the availability of software is likely to change rapidly. Also, if certain software is not mentioned, this does not indicate our disapproval of it.

The assignment consists of tree parts.

1. In the first part, you will create an ontology that describes the domain and contains the information needed by your own application. You will use the terms defined in the ontology to describe concrete data. In this step, you will be applying the methodology for ontology construction outlined in the first part of this chapter, and you will be using OWL as a representation language for your ontology (see chapter 4).

2. In the second part, you will use your ontology to construct different views on your data, and you will query the ontology and the data to extract information needed for each view. In this part, you will be applying RDF storage and querying facilities (see chapter 3).

3. In the third part, you will create different graphic presentations of the extracted data using XSLT technology (see chapter 2).

## Part I. Creating an Ontology

As a first step, you need to decide on an application domain to tackle in your project. Preferably, this is a domain in which you yourself have sufficient knowledge or for which you have easy access to an expert with that knowledge.

In this description of the project, we will use the domain we use in our own course, namely, the domain of a university faculty, with its teachers, courses, and departments, but of course you can replace this with any domain of your own choosing.

Second, you will build an ontology expressed in OWL that describes the domain (for example, your faculty). The ontology does not have to cover the whole domain, but it should contain at least a few dozen classes. Pay special attention to the quality (breadth, depth) of the ontology, and aim to use as much of OWL's expressiveness as possible. There are a number of possible tools to use at this stage. We have good experiences with OILed,[15] but other editors can also be used, e.g., Protégé,[16] or OntoEdit.[17] If you are ambitious, you may even want to start your ontology development using ontology extraction tools from text (but we have no experience with this in our own course), or to experiment with some of the tools that allow you to import semistructured data sources, such as Excell sheets, tab-delimited files, etc. See, for example, Excel2RDF and ConvertToRDF.[18] Of course, you may choose to start from some existing ontologies in this area.[19]

Preferably, also use an inference engine to validate your ontology and check it for inconsistencies. We have experience using the FaCT reasoning engine that is closely coupled with OILed, but OntoEdit has its own inference engine. If you use Protégé, you may want to exploit some of the available

---

15. <http://oiled.man.ac.uk>.
16. <http://protege.stanford.edu>.
17. <http://ontoprise.de>.
18. <http://www.mindswap.org>.
19. For example those found in <http://www.daml.org/ontologies>.

plug-ins for this editor, such as multiple visualizations for your ontology, or reasoning in Prolog or Jess.

Third, you export your ontology in RDF Schema. Of course, this will result in information loss from your rich OWL ontology, but this is inevitable given the limited capabilities of the tools used in subsequent steps, and this is also likely to be a realistic scenario in actual Semantic Web applications.

Finally, you should populate your ontology with concrete instances and their properties. Depending on the choice of editing tool, this can either be done with the same tool (OntoEdit) or will have to be done in another way (OILed). Given the simple syntactic structure of instances in RDF, you may even decide to write these by hand, or to code some simple scripts to extract the instance information from available online sources (in our own course, students got some of the information from the faculty's phonebook). You may want to use the the validation service offered by W3C.[20] This service not only validates your files for syntactic correctness but also provides a visualization of the existing triples. Also, at this stage, you may be able to experiment with some of the tools that allow you to import data from semistructured sources,

At the end of this step, you should be able to produce the following:

- The full OWL ontology

- The reduced version of this ontology as exported to RDF Schema

- The instances of the ontology, described in RDF

- A report describing the scope of the ontology and the main design decisions you have taken during modeling it.

## Part II. Profile Building with RQL Queries

In this step, you will use query facilities to extract certain relevant parts of your ontology and data. For this you will need some way of storing your ontology in a repository that also supports query facilities. You may use the Sesame RDF storage and query facility,[21] but other options exist, such as the KAON server,[22] or JENA.[23]

---

20. <http://www.w3.org /RDF/Validator/>.
21. <http://sesame.aidministrator.nl>.
22. <http://kaon.semanticweb.org>.
23. <http://www.hpl.hp.com/semweb>.

The first step is to upload your ontology (in RDF Schema form) and associated instances to the repository. This may involve some installation effort.

Next, use the query language associated with the repository to define different user profiles and to use queries to extract the data relevant for each profile.

Although these programs support different query languages (RQL for Sesame, RDQL for Jena, KAON Query for the KAON server), they all provide sufficient expressiveness to define rich profiles. In the example of modeling your own faculty, you may, for example, choose to define profiles for students from different years, profiles for students from abroad, profiles for students and teachers, profiles for access over broadband or slow modem-lines, and so on.

The output of the queries that define a profile will typically be in an XML format: RDF/XML, or some other form of XML.

## Part III. Presenting Profile-Based Information

In this final part, use the XML output of the queries from part II to generate a human-readable presentation of the different profiles.

The obvious technology to use in this final part is XML Style Sheets, in particular XSLT (see Chapter 2). A variety of different editors exist for XSLT, as well as a variety of XSLT processors.[24]

The challenge of this part is to define browsable, highly interlinked presentations of the data generated and selected in parts I and II.

## Conclusion

After you have finished all parts of this proposed project, you will effectively have implemented large parts of the architecture shown in figure 7.1. You will have used most of the languages described in this book (XML, XSLT, RDF, RDF Schema, OWL), and you will have built a genuine Semantic Web application: modeling a part of the world in an ontology, using querying to define user-specific views on this ontology, and using XML technology to define browsable presentations of such user-specific views.

---

24. See, for example, <http://www.xslt.com>.

# 8 *Conclusion and Outlook*

## 8.1 How It All Fits Together

At this time it may be instructive to look back at chapter 1, where the Semantic Web vision was described. In this book, we described the key Semantic Web technologies. Now we consider an automated bargaining scenario to see how all technologies discussed fit together.

- Each bargaining party is represented by a *software agent*. We have not discussed agents in this book and refer readers to the extensive literature. Often, agents are treated as black boxes, which solve all problems miraculously. We preferred to concentrate on the internals of agents, and refrained from discussing aspects of agent communication and collaboration.

- The agents need to agree on the meaning of certain terms by committing to a shared *ontology*, e.g., written in OWL.

- Case facts, offers, and decisions can be represented using *RDF statements*. These statements become really useful when linked to an ontology.

- Information is exchanged between the agents in some *XML-based (or RDF-based) language*.

- The agent negotiation strategies are described in a *logical language*.

- An agent decides about the next course of action through *inferring* conclusions from the negotiation strategy, case facts, and previous offers and counteroffers.

## 8.2    Some Technical Questions

### 8.2.1    Web Ontology Language: Is Less More?

Much of the effort in Semantic Web research has gone into developing an appropriate Web ontology language, resulting in OWL as the current standard. One key question is whether the ontology languages need to be very complex. While one can always think of cases that one might wish to model and that are beyond the expressive power of full first-order logic, the question remains whether these issues are important *in practice*.

There are reasons to expect that most ontological knowledge will be of a rather simple nature, and that less expressive languages will be sufficient. The advantages of simple ontology languages are a more efficient reasoning support, a simpler language for tool vendors to support, and a more easily usable language. The latter may turn out to be of crucial importance for the success of the Semantic Web. OWL Lite is a step in the right direction.

### 8.2.2    Rules and Ontologies

As we said in chapter 4, the current (advanced) Web ontology languages are based on description logics. On the other hand, it has been recognized that rules are an important and simple representation formalism with many applications. Currently there is ongoing work on combining both.

We believe that a formalism that combines the full power of both description logics and rules would be overkill. Apart from questions regarding the need for such rich languages, the research has revealed several complexity and computability barriers that are difficult to overcome.

A sensible compromise approach may be to take RDFS and put rules on top, as an alternative to going down the path of description logics. There are no real technical problems with this approach. And it is not as restrictive as it looks, because many features of description logics (and thus OWL) are definable using rules.

## 8.3    Predicting the Future

So, will the Semantic Web initiative succeed? While many people believe in it (and in fact are investing in it), the outcome is still open. As suggested at the beginning of this book, the question is not so much a technological but rather a practical one: Will we be able to demonstrate the usefulness of this technology quickly and powerfully enough to create momentum (recreating something similar to the early stages of the World Wide Web)?

*Where will the ontologies come from?*  We already see the solutions to this potential bottleneck: some large ontologies are becoming de facto standards (WordNet, NCIBI's cancer ontology), and many small ontologies are either hand-created by organizations (e.g., RosettaNet) or by machine through machine learning techniques, natural language analysis, and borrowing from legacy resources (e.g., database schemas).

*Where will the semantic markup come from?*  It is clear that the bulk of the required large volumes of semantic markup will not be created by hand (unlike the start of the World Wide Web, which did happen through hand-coded HTML pages).  Instead, analysis of documents through natural language techniques and borrowing from legacy sources (e.g., databases) will be prominent techniques here.

*Where will the tools come from?*  This is a potential bottleneck that is already in the process of being resolved.  A large variety of tools is already available for every aspect of the Semantic Web application life cycle (editors, storage, query and inference infrastructure, visualization, versioning tools).  Currently these tools are mostly in the academic domain, but they are quickly being taken up by the commercial sector, in particular, by highly innovative startups, both in the United States and in the European Union.

*How should one deal with a multitude of ontologies?*  This problem (known as the ontology mapping problem) is perhaps the hardest problem to be solved.  Many approaches are being investigated (based on negotiating agents, machine learning, or linguistic analysis), but the jury is still out on this one.

Possibly the first success stories will not emerge in the open heterogeneous environment of the WWW but rather in intranets of large organizations.  In such environments, central control may impose the use of standards and technologies, and possibly the first real success stories will emerge.  Thus we believe that *knowledge management* for large organizations may be the most promising area to start.

Other areas that will be quick to follow are so-called e-science: the use of the Semantic Web by scientists (just as the use by scientists was an important catalyst for the World Wide Web).  It could well be that e-commerce, with all its associated problems of privacy, security, and trust, will only be a later application of the Semantic Web.

All in all, we are optimistic about the future of the Semantic Web and hope that this book as a teaching resource will play its role in "bringing the Web to its full potential".

# A Abstract OWL Syntax

The XML syntax for OWL, as we have used it in chapter 4 is rather verbose, and hard to read. OWL also has an abstract syntax[1], which is much easier to read.

This appendix lists the abstract syntax for all the OWL code discussed in chapter 4.

### 4.2.2: Header

```
Ontology(
 Annotation(rdfs:comment "An example OWL ontology")
 Annotation(rdfs:label "University Ontology")
 Annotation(owl:imports http://www.mydomain.org/persons)
)
```

### 4.2.3: Class Elements

```
Class(associateProfessor partial academicStaffMember)

Class(professor partial)
DisjointClasses(associateProfessor assistantProfessor)
DisjointClasses(professor associateProfessor)

Class(faculty complete academicStaffMember)
```

---

1. Defined in <http://www.w3.org/TR/owl-semantics/>

### 4.2.4: Property Elements

```
DatatypeProperty(age range(xsd:nonNegativeInteger))

ObjectProperty(isTaughtBy
  domain(course)
  range(academicStaffMember))
SubPropertyOf(isTaughtBy involves)

ObjectProperty(teaches
  inverseOf(isTaughtBy)
  domain(academicStaffMember)
  range(course))

ObjectProperty(lecturesIn)
EquivalentProperties(lecturesIn teaches)
```

### 4.2.5: Property Restrictions

```
Class(firstYearCourse partial
  restriction(isTaughtBy allValuesFrom (Professor)))

Class(mathCourse partial
  restriction(isTaughtBy hasValue (949352)))

Class(academicStaffMember partial
  restriction(teaches someValuesFrom (undergraduateCourse)))

Class(course partial
  restriction(isTaughtBy minCardinality(1)))

Class(department partial
  restriction(hasMember minCardinality(10))
  restriction(hasMember maxCardinality(30)))
```

### 4.2.6: Special Properties

```
ObjectProperty(hasSameGradeAs Transitive Symmetric
  domain(student)
  range(student))
```

### 4.2.7: Boolean Combinations

```
Class(course partial
  complementOf(staffMember))

Class(peopleAtUni complete
  unionOf(staffMember student))

Class(facultyInCS complete
  intersectionOf(faculty
                 restriction(belongsTo
                             hasValue
                             (CSDepartment)))))

Class(adminStaff complete
  intersectionOf(staffMember
                 complementOf(unionOf(faculty
                                      techSupportStaff)))))
```

### 4.2.8: Enumerations

```
EnumeratedClass(weekdays Monday
                        Tuesday
                        Wednesday
                        Thursday
                        Friday
                        Saturday
                        Sunday)
```

### 4.2.9: Instances

```
Individual(949352
  type(academicStaffMember))

Individual(949352
  type(academicStaffMember)
  value(age "39"^^&xsd;integer))

ObjectProperty(isTaughtBy Functional)

Individual(CIT1111
  type(course)
```

```
  value(isTaughtBy 949352)
  value(isTaughtBy 949318))

Individual(949318
 type(lecturer))
DifferentIndividuals(949318 949352)

DifferentIndividuals(949352 949111 949318)
```

## 4.3.1: African Wildlife Ontology

```
Ontology(

ObjectProperty(eaten-by inverseOf(eats))
ObjectProperty(eats domain(animal))
ObjectProperty(is-part-of Transitive)

Class(animal partial
 annotation(rdfs:comment "Animals form a class."))

Class(branch partial
 annotation(rdfs:comment "Branches are parts of trees.")
 restriction(is-part-of allValuesFrom (tree)))

Class(carnivore complete
 annotation(rdfs:comment
             "Carnivores are exactly those animals that eat
              animals.")
  intersectionOf(animal
                  restriction(eats someValuesFrom (animal))))

Class(giraffe partial
 annotation(rdfs:comment
             "Giraffes are herbivores,
              and they eat only leaves.")
  herbivore
  restriction(eats allValuesFrom (leaf)))

Class(herbivore complete
 annotation(rdfs:comment
             "Herbivores are exactly those animals that
              eat only plants or parts of plants.")
```

```
        intersectionOf(
             animal
             restriction(eats
                          allValuesFrom
                          (unionOf(plant
                                   restriction(is-part-of
                                               allValuesFrom
                                               (plant)))))))

Class(leaf partial
 annotation(rdfs:comment "Leaves are parts of branches.")
 restriction(is-part-of allValuesFrom (branch)))

Class(lion partial
 annotation(rdfs:comment
             "Lions are animals that eat only herbivores.")
 carnivore
 restriction(eats allValuesFrom (herbivore)))

Class(plant partial
 annotation(rdfs:comment
             "Plants form a class disjoint from animals."))

Class(tasty-plant partial
 annotation(rdfs:comment
             "Tasty plants are plants that are eaten
              both by herbivores and carnivores.")
 plant
 restriction(eaten-by someValuesFrom (herbivore))
 restriction(eaten-by someValuesFrom (carnivore)))


Class(tree partial
 annotation(rdfs:comment "Trees are a type of plant.")
 plant)

AnnotationProperty(rdfs:comment)
DisjointClasses(plant animal)
)
```

### 4.3.2: Printer Ontology

```
Ontology(

 Annotation(owl:versionInfo
             "My example version 1.2, 17 October 2002")

 DatatypeProperty(manufactured-by
  domain(product)
  range(xsd:string))

 DatatypeProperty(price
  domain(product)
  range(xsd:nonNegativeInteger))

 DatatypeProperty(printingResolution
  domain(printer)
  range(xsd:string))

 DatatypeProperty(printingSpeed
  domain(printer)
  range(xsd:string))

 DatatypeProperty(printingTechnology
  domain(printer)
  range(xsd:string))

 Class(1100se partial
  annotation(rdfs:comment
              "1100se printers belong to the 1100 series
               and cost $450.")
  1100series
  restriction(price hasValue ("450"^^&xsd;integer)))

 Class(1100series partial
  annotation(rdfs:comment
              "1100series printers are HP laser jet
               printers with 8ppm printing speed and 600dpi
               printing resolution.")
  hpLaserJetPrinter
  restriction(printingSpeed hasValue ("8ppm"^^&xsd;string))
  restriction(printingResolution
```

```
                  hasValue ("600dpi"^^&xsd;string)))

Class(1100xi partial
 annotation(rdfs:comment
               "1100xi printers belong to the 1100 series
                and cost $350.")
 1100series
 restriction(price hasValue ("350"^^&xsd;integer)))

Class(hpLaserJetPrinter partial
 annotation(rdfs:comment
               "HP laser jet printers are HP products
                and laser jet printers.")
 laserJetPrinter
 hpPrinter)

Class(hpPrinter partial
 annotation(rdfs:comment
               "HP printers are  HP products and printers.")
 hpProduct
 printer)

Class(hpProduct complete
 annotation(rdfs:comment
               "HP products are exactly those products
                that are manufactured by Hewlett Packard.")
 intersectionOf(
     product
     restriction(manufactured-by
                 hasValue ("Hewlett Packard"^^&xsd;string))))

Class(laserJetPrinter complete
 annotation(rdfs:comment
               "Laser jet printers are exactly those printers
                that use laser jet printing technology.")
 intersectionOf(
     printer
     restriction(printingTechnology
                 hasValue ("laser jet"^^&xsd;string))))

Class(padid partial
 annotation(rdfs:comment
```

```
                    "Printing and digital imaging devices
                     form a subclass of products.")
      annotation(rdfs:label "Device")
      product)

    Class(personalPrinter partial
      annotation(rdfs:comment "Printers for personal use form
                               a subclass of printers.")
      printer)

    Class(printer partial
      annotation(rdfs:comment "Printers are printing and
                               digital imaging devices.")
      padid)

    Class(product partial
      annotation(rdfs:comment "Products form a class."))
  )
```

# Index